To

Norman

In Vino Veritas

Kenny Walker

1001
Questions & Answers
About
WINE

ABOUT THE AUTHOR

Henry Walker holds a bachelor's degree in marketing from New York University and a master's degree in English from Jersey City State College. His working life has been spent in the alcoholic beverage industry, with particular emphasis on wine. He has been a sales representative for a leading liquor company, an independent broker, and an executive with a prominent winery. He is now associated with Joseph H. Reinfeld, Inc., one of America's largest importers and wholesalers. He has conducted innumerable wine tastings, trade seminars and sales training sessions. In the wine trade he is a sought-after speaker and consultant. *1001 Questions and Answers About Wine* is the culmination of years of research, sampling and professional experience.

HENRY WALKER

1001
Questions & Answers
About
WINE

LYLE STUART, INC.
Secaucus, N. J.

First edition
Copyright © 1976 by Henry Walker

Published by Lyle Stuart, Inc. Published simultaneously in Canada by George J. McLeod Limited, 73 Bathurst St., Toronto, Ont.

Manufactured in the United States of America

LIBRARY OF CONGRESS CATALOGING IN PUBLICATION

Walker, Henry, 1927-
    1001 questions and answers about wine.

    Includes index.
    1. Wine and wine making. I. Title.
TP548.W294   641.2'2   75-44499
ISBN 0-8184-0214-8

TO MARJORIE

*with whom I have shared
many a glass of wine,
as well as many of life's other joys*

Foreword

Wine. Many aspects of the subject involve hair-splitting technicalities that, in the final analysis, are of no great consequence. To become obsessed with trifles would result in a pedantic work.

Moreover, every year sees some minor revisions in some of the practices and regulations dealing with the production and distribution of wine.

All this notwithstanding, 1001 *Questions and Answers about Wine* is as factually correct, up-to-date, and informative as any wine book can possibly be.

In the early days of my interest in wine, the more I read, the more confused I became. Most of the literature I found (and my search was exhaustive) was virtually meaningless to me as a neophyte.

This book was written with the lay person uppermost in mind. The approach is fundamental, the format is easy to follow, and the terminology is nontechnical.

There is no need to be a "walking encyclopedia" to

enjoy a glass of wine. Nor is it a prerequisite to have an extraordinary sense of taste—few people actually do.

First, try to acquire a measure of basic information about the subject. Then, over a period of time and at your own pace, sample a broad variety of different kinds of wine. You will be pleasantly surprised at how quickly you will develop confidence in your own reactions and judgments.

Read.   Drink.   Enjoy!

1001
Questions & Answers
About
WINE

Index begins on page 239

1

What is wine?

The fermented juice of grapes, berries, or other fruit.

2

What is the purpose of fermentation?

To impart alcoholic content to the extract.

3

How much alcohol will fermentation impart?

Between 7 and 14 percent by volume.

4

Is percent by volume the same as proof?

No; 1 percent by volume is equal to two proof. A 7 percent wine is the equivalent of 14 proof, and a 14 percent wine is the equivalent of 28 proof.

5

What kind of alcohol results from fermentation?

Ethyl alcohol.

6

Is this the same kind of alcohol that is found in beer and whiskey?

Yes. Ethyl alcohol is present in all alcoholic beverages. Fermentation, as in beer and wine, will induce a limited level of concentration. Greater potency may be obtained through distillation, a series of boiling procedures.

7

What causes fermentation?

All fruits have some degree of natural sugar. When pure fruit juice is exposed to air and cultured yeast cells, the enzymes in the yeast trigger a chemical action that converts the sugar elements into ethyl alcohol.

8

What kind of sugar is grape sugar?

Levulose, glucose, and dextrose.

9

Can the period of fermentation be lengthened to increase the alcoholic concentration?

No. Each grape, fruit, or berry variety has its own individual peak of fermentation somewhere between 7 and 14 percent alcohol by volume. Fermentation will cease of its own accord when the levulose, glucose, and dextrose have been transformed into ethyl alcohol.

10

Does this mean that wine can never be stronger than 14 percent by volume?

No. Potency may be elevated by adding neutral, distilled, or grape spirits.

11

If all grapes contain sugar, shouldn't all wines be sweet?

No. Much of the sugar is transformed into ethyl alcohol during fermentation. Some grape varieties will leave some sugar residue, but never an overpowering, cloying, saturated, or syrupy solution.

12

What is a dry wine?

One that lacks pronounced sweetness.

13

Are all dry wines lacking in sweetness to the same extent?

No. Some are quite tart. Others have a mild suggestion of sweetness and are properly referred to as semi-dry wines.

14

Are dry wines the same as table wines?

Yes. The terms are interchangeable. Dry, or table, wines are those which have been traditionally associated with food.

15

What are some examples of dry wines?

Burgundy, Chianti, Rosé, Sauterne, Liebfraumilch, Chablis, Rhine.

16

Are table wines classified by color?

Yes. Three classifications have been established—red, white, and rosé.

17

Do these classifications truly indicate the wine's color?

Not really. Reds can run from pale pink to deep purple. Whites can include tints extending from clear liquid to deep amber. Rosés can encompass shades of red, crimson, or pink.

18

How many basic color categories are there for grapes?

Two—red and white. Red also includes varieties that are actually black or blue. White includes yellow and green varieties as well.

19

Does the color of the grapes determine the color of the wine?

No. It is 99 percent accurate to say that pure grape juice is a colorless liquid, regardless of the color of the grapes.

20

Can any color of wine be made from any color of grapes?

Whites can. Reds and rosés, however, require red, blue, or black grapes because the skins of green and yellow grapes are too pale.

21

Is grape wine artificially colored?

Color additives are rarely used. The color is almost always the natural color of the skins, especially with dry reds and rosés. The ultimate tint is largely influenced by the color of the skins and the length of time the skins are combined with the liquid extract during fermentation.

22

What is the technical name for the process of combining juice and skins?

The process is called *cuvaison*.

23

Do skins play any other roles in vinification?

Yes, two very important roles. Skins harbor natural yeast cells, which aid in fermentation. They also contain natural acids, oils, and benevolent bacteria that are vital to dry wines.

24

How long do the skins remain in contact with the liquid extract?

From two days to two weeks for a rosé or light-tinted red. Up to thirty days for a deep-tinted red.

25

What acid compounds are present in wine?

Tannic, tartaric, and malic acids. These are essential in vinifying dry wines, particularly dry red wines.

26

Are stalks used in making wine?

No. Stalks are removed and discarded, since they are devoid of any salutary natural properties.

27

Do grape leaves have any vinification value?

None whatever.

28

Can fermentation be artificially stimulated?

No. No synthesized or manufactured chemical substance can take the place of natural or cultured yeast cells.

29

What physical activity takes place during fermentation?

Fermentation is characterized by liquid agitation and turbulence. The liquid bubbles and churns furiously.

30

What is malolactic fermentation?

Juices rich in malic acid have a tendency to nurture micro-organisms that yield strains of lactic acid. This chemical alteration gives off a few milligrams of carbon dioxide, which can be captured to endow the wine with a soft effervescence.

31

What is free-run juice?

The luscious juice that is released through a light squeezing of the grapes, as opposed to a forceful, vigorous pressing. Free-run juice is described as the nectar, or "heart and soul," of the grape. An analogy might be drawn between free-run juice and the first tender bite of a piece of rich, succulent fruit.

32

Is there a special name for the juice undergoing fermentation?

Yes. It is called *must*.

33

Do wine grapes have seeds?

Black, blue, and red grapes do. Most green and yellow grapes are seedless.

34

Are the seeds left intact during fermentation?

Yes. The turbulence caused by fermentation forces the seeds, or *pips* as they are called, to the surface, where they can be easily scooped out of the vat when fermentation is complete.

35

Do seeds have any vinification value?

Yes. Seeds contain natural acids that lend body to the wine. Seeds also embody natural oils that precipitate droplets of glycerine, a natural bouquet booster.

36

Is there a common name for wines stronger than 14 percent by volume?

Yes. They are known as *sweet, dessert,* or *fortified* wines.

37

What are some examples of sweet wines?

Port, Sherry, and Muscatel.

38

How is wine fortified?

A distillate made from grain (neutral spirits) or grapes (brandy) is added to the liquid.

39

How does fortification impart sweetness?

The introduction of spirits or brandy causes fermentation to cease. That proportion of the sugar remaining in the must invests the liquid with sweetness.

40

How long does the fermentation cycle last?

In dessert vinification, fermentation may be intentionally arrested after anywhere from two to ten weeks. In dealing with dry wines, protracted or full-cycle fermentation is encouraged. Depending on the grape variety, total or near-total "fermenting out" may take as long as six months.

41

Is temperature control necessary during fermentation?

Yes. Extreme heat or cold or sudden temperature changes can cause fermentation to cease abruptly. Once arrested because of temperature factors, fermentation may be difficult to reactivate.

42

Is it necessary to control air quality during fermentation?

Yes. Impurities in the atmosphere can cause the must to manufacture acetic acid, a component of vinegar that can render the liquid disagreeably sour.

43

Is fermentation ever arrested in vinifying table wines?

Yes. Some table wines are more pleasant and enjoyable as semi-dry, rather than austerely dry, beverages. A touch of residual sugar may be retained by arresting fermentation when it is, say, 80, 85, or 90 percent complete.

44

How is fermentation arrested in vinifying semi-dry wines?

The arresting agent is sulfur dioxide. Handling this gaseous substance demands vinification expertise, because overt evidence of sulphur in the finished product can detract from its taste.

45

Are there gradations in the sweetness of Sherry?

Yes. In ascending order of sweetness: cocktail, pale dry, dry, medium, regular, straight, and cream. These are arbitrary gradations that apply only to American Sherry.

46

Are there gradations in the sweetness of Port?

Yes. Tawny Port is less sweet than Ruby Port.

47

Are there any fixed standards governing the sweetness of dessert wines?

No. Each vintner sets his own guidelines. Thus, a given brand of Pale Dry Sherry or Ruby Port may be less sweet or more sweet than another.

48

What sort of vessel is best for aging dry wine?

Wooden barrels are gradually being replaced by glass-lined cement or ceramic cylinders and stainless-steel tanks. It is easier to clean the interior of a non-porous vessel.

49

How long is a dry wine aged?

Usually from less than one year to more than five years.

50

In dry wines, does longer aging yield superior quality?

Not necessarily. Most whites reach their peak of maturity sooner than most reds—sometimes in one-third to one-half as much time. Red or white, however, some grape varieties fare best as young wines, while others demand a much longer aging period for full development.

51

What is the consequence of inadequate aging?

Depending on the grape variety, the wine may be rough, coarse, or deficient in the taste and flavor traits most desirable for its type.

52

Can a dry wine suffer from too much aging?

Definitely. A dry wine that is delightfully ready for bottling at sixteen months may lose much of its intrinsic charm and appeal if aged for, say, twenty-nine months. The key to perfection lies in recognizing when the optimum plane of maturity for a particular grape variety, or combination of varieties, has been reached.

53

Must the age of a wine be stated on the label?

No. Packaging laws make no provision for mention of how long the wine matured in a barrel or cask after fermentation. To provide this information for every type of wine would be utterly meaningless and hopelessly confusing.

54

Do table wines improve with age in the bottle?

Some do. Extremely high-bred reds seem to attain their peak from four to eight years after they have been bottled. The controlling factor is the presence of tannin (tannic acid). The more tannin, the more time the wine takes to arrive at the peak of perfection.

55

Are some dry wines supposed to have a sour taste?

Never. Unsweet, crisp, tart, astringent—yes. But sour —never. Such a taste sensation is a sign of a defect in the wine itself.

56

How many different varieties of grapes are there?

It is impossible to fix a precise number. Hundreds have been catalogued, but thousands are in bloom owing to mixed plantings, cross-cultivation, and hybrid growths.

57

Can all varieties of grapes be universally cultivated?

No. There are too many physical variables. Some grape varieties need chalky soil; some, a prolonged span of warm weather; some, proximity to a body of water; some, mountainous terrain.

58

Is good soil a prerequisite for good grapes?

Grapes may thrive in sandy, rocky, chalky, volcanic, slate-laden, gravel-heavy soil that would impede the growth of other crops. Such soil may possess minerals and chemicals and drainage peculiarities that are singularly beneficial to certain classes of vines.

59

How much wine will an acre of grapes produce?

From slightly more than one hundred cases to almost one thousand cases.

60

Is there a correlation between quantity and quality?

At either extreme, yes. Some of the world's most celebrated and most expensive wines come from vineyards where the yield is less than 125 cases per acre. Acreage that is densely planted or overrun with vines seldom generates an end product of outstanding caliber.

61

Must a winery cultivate its own grapes?

No. It would be impossible for a major winery to satisfy its entire needs internally. Homegrown inventory is augmented by purchases from independent farmers and agricultural cooperatives.

62

Do some vineyards grow only one variety?

Yes. Some European districts confine their production to a handful of species. Some vineyards within the district may specialize in a single variety.

63

How long can a vineyard remain fertile?

Almost forever if the soil is painstakingly cared for, if there is no dramatic change in the composition of the subsoil, and if there is no disastrous upheaval in climatic conditions. Some American vineyards are more than a hundred years old. Some European vineyards are still going strong after five centuries.

64

How long does it take to germinate a new vineyard?

New acreage will bloom in two to four years with favorable soil and weather conditions and dedicated care.

65

How often are vines pruned?

Vines of any worth at all must be cut and trimmed seasonally. Premium varieties are pruned with a free and liberal hand. The root of the stock is the primary source of sustenance. The fewer clusters of grapes that feed off each root, the better—the more root nutriment per cluster.

66

Do wine grapes look the same as table grapes?

Premium wine grapes would look unattractive and uninviting in the produce department of a supermarket. They are much smaller than table grapes and have an over-ripe, dried-out appearance.

67

What is a still wine?

One that is neither carbonated, crackling, sparkling, nor effervescent.

68

Does this mean that a still wine never has any bubbles?

Not always. Some still wines have a mild tingle or slight effervescence due to their retention of natural gases.

69

When is the best time to harvest grapes?

As late as possible in the fall. Grapes stop growing toward the end of summer. Between then and the onset of cold weather, grapes ripen to their fullest degree of flavor, bouquet, and natural sugar content.

70

Some fruits become moldy when overripe. Do grapes?

Positively. Therein lies one of the secrets of excellent wine. The mold that forms on the skins is cherished as "noble mold" or "noble rot." These bacterial fungi serve to heighten flavor intensity, especially with semidry white wines.

71

Is there a relationship between the alcohol content and the quality of a dry wine?

No. The traditional theory that insists upon 12 to 14 percent as a criterion is fast becoming discredited. The critical consideration is the wine's character. A wine that is vinified as a full-bodied, rich, robust beverage would of course be noticeably vapid at 7 or 9 percent. By the same token, a wine that is supposed to be on the light-bodied, delicate side would be disappointingly harsh at 13 percent.

72

What is a generic wine?

A non-European wine that takes its name from a European district. Burgundy, Chablis, Sauterne, Rhine, Port (Oporto), and Sherry (Jerez) are generic wines. The non-European version bears some family resemblance to the European original.

73

May natural flavoring agents be added to wine?

Yes. Some wines are vinified as flavored beverages and are so labeled.

74

Are fruit-flavored wines artificially colored?

They may be. Certified coloring, a synthesized food or vegetable derivative, is permissible when *cuvaison* results in inadequate or inappropriate coloring.

75

What are some of the more popular types of fruit-flavored wines?

Cherry, strawberry, apple, blackberry, elderberry, loganberry.

76

What is a "100 percent pure" wine?

Fruit-flavored bottlings may be so labeled to guarantee that the wine was made from natural fruit juices rather than chemical substitutes. With grape wines the notation would be superfluous.

77

What is a "pop" wine?

An inexpensive wine vinified with a fruit base or natural flavor additives and mass marketed with an ethnic or young-adult accent. Most "pop" wines are low in alcohol content and are imaginatively named, for promotional purposes.

78

What is an aperitif?

A wine that is an ideal before-dinner or cocktail beverage. Aperitifs are flavored with botanicals, herbs, and spices and are usually fortified.

79

Can Vermouth be consumed as an aperitif?

Definitely. The popularity of vermouth as an aperitif is beginning to rival its use in Martinis and Manhattans.

80

What gives Vermouth its distinctive taste?

Essences concocted from petals, leaves, peels, stems, roots, barks, herbs, and spices are steeped in the base liquid. The interplay of these flavoring agents imbues Vermouth with unique sensory dimensions.

81

What kind of base wine is used for Vermouth?

A bland white for Dry Vermouth and a thin red for Sweet Vermouth. While the base wines have a bearing on the tint of the finished beverage, the sensory properties accrue from the vintner's private recipe.

82

Why is Dry Vermouth called French *and Sweet Vermouth* Italian?

Because they were conceived in these countries. Both kinds are now vinified in both countries and in the United States.

83

How much alcohol does Vermouth contain?

Between 17 and 21 percent by volume. Even the so-called dry version is fortified.

84

Is wine pasteurized?

Only low-grade wines are pasteurized. Heat kills impurities but it also kills compatible bacteria that enable the wine to continue to develop and improve.

85

What are lees?

Fruit solids that accumulate during vinification. The lees are separated from the liquid when the wine is transferred from one vessel to another for aging and storage.

86

What is meant by fining a wine?

The withdrawal of any grape particles, foreign deposits, or impurities that may be suspended in the final liquid. The fining material is usually a clear, unflavored gelatin that absorbs unwanted matter and then settles at the bottom of the vat.

87

By what other method can impurities be removed?

Through the slower, more exacting means of repeated straining and filtering before bottling.

88

Can an individual bottling consist of the fermented juices of different kinds of grapes?

Definitely. A number of wines, American and imported, are made from a combination of juices. Skillful blending is of tremendous benefit in creating the most desirable flavor balance for many bottlings.

89

What is a proprietary wine?

One that is the exclusive trademark, property, or formulation of a single supplier.

90

How many ounces are there in a fifth?

25.6 ounces. A fifth is one-fifth of a gallon, or four-fifths of a quart.

91

What is a split?

A wine measure equivalent to one-quarter of a fifth, or 6.4 ounces. A split is also called a twentieth.

92

What is a tenth?

A wine measure equivalent to one-half of a fifth, or 12.8 ounces. A tenth is also called a half-bottle.

93

What is a magnum?

A wine measure equivalent to 2 fifths, or 51.2 ounces.

94

What wine measures are based on the quart?

½ pint	¼ quart	8 ounces
pint	½ quart	16 ounces
½ gallon	2 quarts	64 ounces
gallon	4 quarts	128 ounces

95

How many ounces in a liter?

33.8 ounces. Imported wines may be bottled in liters or in other non-American sizes such as 18, 18.6, 20, 23, 24, 40, 59, and 60 ounces.

96

Has the metric system gained official support in this country?

Yes. Metric measurements will be mandatory for all wines entering trade channels here starting January 1, 1979. The following seven sizes have been legally sanctioned:

3	liters	101.4 ounces	(101.46)
1½	liters	50.7 ounces	(50.73)
1	liter	33.8 ounces	(33.82)
¾	liter	25.4 ounces	(25.36)
⅜	liter	12.7 ounces	(12.68)
3⁄16	liter	6.3 ounces	(6.34)
⅒	liter	3.4 ounces	(3.38)

97

Are table wines and fortified wines subject to the same federal tax?

No. Wines not in excess of 14 percent alcohol by volume are taxed at the rate of seventeen cents per gallon. The rate jumps to sixty-seven cents a gallon for fortified wines.

98

Does each state levy an additional tax?

Yes. State excise taxes vary from 2½ cents to two dollars per gallon.

99

What is the legal limit for alcohol content?

24 percent by volume.

100

Does alcohol content appear on the label?

Yes. This is mandatory under federal regulations.

101

Can the alcohol content change in the bottle?

No. Physical or chemical changes that may occur in the bottle have no effect on alcohol content.

102

Can a California wine be made from grapes grown elsewhere?

No. A California wine must be made entirely from grapes harvested within the state.

103

What is a California varietal wine?

One that bears the name of the specific grape variety from which the wine was principally made.

104

What are the leading California varietal wines?

Red wines:

Barbera
Charbono
Cabernet Sauvignon
Gamay Beaujolais
Petite Sirah
Pinot Noir
Zinfandel

White wines:

Chenin Blanc
Folle Blanche
Gewürztraminer
Grey Riesling
Johannisberg Riesling
Pinot Blanc
Pinot Chardonnay
Sauvignon Blanc
Sémillon
Sylvaner
Sylvaner Riesling
Traminer

Rose wines:

Grenache
Gamay
Grignolino

105

What is the origin of California varietal grapes?
They are of French, German, or Italian descent.

106

Do these grape varieties still bloom in Europe?
Yes, with the exception of Zinfandel. The precise
history of this variety is speculative. It is theorized that the
original stock was brought from Europe more than a
century ago. Nowhere on the continent, however, has any
single variety been credited as the progenitor of Zinfandel.

107

*Are varietal grapes of higher caliber than the stock from
which generic wines are vinified?*
On an overall plane of comparison, yes. Collectively,
these grapes yield some of America's finest table wines.

108

Are varietal grapes extensively planted?
No. They account for less than seven percent of California's output.

109

Which varietal is the most prolific bloomer?
Zinfandel. It has been estimated that Zinfandel output
averages 25 to 30 percent of the total varietal yield.

Where are California's varietal vineyards?

In the coastal region above and below San Francisco. With the exception of Zinfandel acreage, varietal vineyards are virtually nonexistent in central and southern California.

Must a California varietal wine be vinified wholly from the grape species for which it is named?

No. Federal law stipulates that a minimum of 51 percent of the identified variety must be used in making the wine.

Must the exact varietal percentage be shown on the table?
No.

Which California varietal wines occupy a special place of distinction?

In the reds, top honors would go to Cabernet Sauvignon or Pinot Noir. In the whites, it would be a tossup between Johannisberg Riesling and Pinot Chardonnay.

Which California varietal wine exhibits the broadest range of quality?

Zinfandel, which can be either undistinguished or superb.

115

Is the exact source of a California varietal bottling always indicated?

No. A specific subdivision of the Northern Coastal region may be shown only when at least 75 percent of the grapes were harvested there. A Cabernet Sauvignon, for example, may be more definitively labeled as a Napa Valley Cabernet Sauvignon if a minimum of three-fourths of its juice was extracted from grapes grown in the Napa Valley. In practice, this legal qualification is sometimes difficult to meet. Varietal acreage is in short supply. Some of the larger wineries in the northern coastal region have had to acquire tracts in more than one district.

116

What are vinifera vines?

Vines of European ancestry that are vinified into table wines. California varietal grapes belong to the vinefera family, also called *Vitis vinefera.*

117

What are labrusca grapes?

Native American varieties found in New York State, especially in the Finger Lakes district, and in the Great Lakes area of the midwest.

118

Which varieties are recognized as labrusca grapes?

Catawba, Clinton, Concord, Delaware, Diamond, Diana, Dutchess, Elvira, Iona, Isabella, Ives, Niagara, Norton, and Vergennes.

119

Is proximity to water advantageous for cultivating labrusca vines?

Yes. These vines flourish best along the shores of large bodies of fresh water. Most labruscas are sturdy, thick-skinned grapes that benefit from exposure to cold air during the ripening months of August and September. At the same time there is a need to protect the vines from premature frosts which can occur around the Finger Lakes and the Great Lakes. The early-morning vapors that rise from the water act as a natural "smudgepot."

120

Which labrusca varieties are the most prolific?

Concord and Catawba. Together they comprise probably one-half of New York State's annual harvest. Concord wine comes in red and white; Catawba in red, pink, and white. Both are the sweetest of all New York State unfortified wines.

121

Do labrusca grapes have a common taste denominator?

Yes. Most labruscas have a noticeable grapy accent, as opposed to the subtle, delicate quality of most viniferas.

122

What viticultural term describes the grapy taste of labrusca grapes?

Labruscas are said to be *foxy.*

123

Is foxiness a viticultural liability?

It depends on the type of bottling. Concord and Catawba wines, for instance, owe much of their appeal to their grapy overtones. Without foxiness, both wines would be rather insipid. Foxiness is less desirable if the result sought is a fine table wine.

124

Is foxiness the same as fruitiness?

No. Foxiness has to do with taste. Fruitiness involves the sense of smell. A fruity wine has a generous trace of fragrance and bouquet. Dry red wines that reach their peak of maturity in less than two years usually have a fruity characteristic.

125

What are French-American hybrid grapes?

Cross-plantings that fuse vines from France with labrusca vines. The viticultural object is to propagate new species a little softer than Concord, Catawba, and other native growths. Many of New York State's better table wines are made with French-American hybrid grapes.

126

What is an estate-bottled wine?

In theory, one that was packaged on the same property where the grapes were grown. In practice, a nominal quantity of the grapes may be purchased from independent growers.

127

What is a "produced and bottled by" bottling?

An American wine in which at least 75 percent of the content was vinified on the bottler's premises or 75 percent of the grape stock harvested on his property.

128

What is a "made and bottled by" bottling?

An American wine in which between 10 and 74 percent of the content was vinified on the bottler's premises or between 10 and 74 percent of the grape stock harvested on his property.

129

Are these designations a valid guide to quality?

Hardly. Some poor wines are estate-bottled. Some marvelous wines are "made and bottled by" wines. In the final analysis, quality is determined by the grade of the grapes and the expertise of the supplier.

130

What is a "bottled by" bottling?

One in which the supplier's function is that of a packaging house rather than a producer. The wine is bought in bulk on the open market and bottled by the supplier under his own trade name.

131

What is a "bottled for" bottling?

A wine put up by a packaging house or bottling establishment as a retailer's private or exclusive label. A "bottled for" package is usually an inexpensive California wine.

132

Do phrases such as specially selected *or* special selection *have any special meaning?*

No legal meaning. Some American suppliers use such terminology when a given wine is felt to be a cut above average. These phrases have been so overworked that their consumer impact is debatable.

133
Does the word château *have any special meaning on an American wine label?*

None whatever.

134
Does the hue of a dry wine change with bottle age?

Sometimes. After three to five years in the bottle, a dry red may begin to turn a trifle paler and a dry white a trifle darker.

135
What is meant by a clean wine?

One that is crystal clear and totally free from deposits, sediment, or cloudy swirls.

136
What is meant by vintage?

The year in which the grapes were harvested.

137
Why do fortified wines seldom bear a vintage inscription?

Because the year in which the grapes were harvested is of scant consequence. The majority of Sherry and Port bottlings are blends of several vintages.

138
Why do comparatively few American wines carry a vintage inscription?

Because the year of the harvest is not a paramount concern in American viticulture. Drastic fluctuations in conditions that influence the harvest are uncommon. Some California varietals and Finger Lakes bottlings do show a vintage year. But whether two different vintages of the same type and brand are dramatically dissimilar is subject to question.

139

Is the vintage year important for German wines?

Not in any significant sense. In top-notch German wines the vintage is not nearly so informative as the identity of the vineyard or the manner in which the grapes were gathered.

140

How meaningful is a vintage notation for Spanish wines?

Not very. Conditions that influence the harvest are fairly stable from year to year.

141

Is the vintage year crucial in evaluating Italian wines?

Not to any great extent. The year in which the grapes were picked is a minor issue. Even a professional wine taster would be hard put to tell one vintage from another.

142

How do some other wine-producing countries look upon vintage designations?

In an incidental, matter-of-fact fashion. In Chile, Argentina, Portugal, Yugoslavia, Hungary, and elsewhere the year of the harvest is largely taken for granted, with no extraordinary emphasis upon "special" years.

143

Why do so many imported French wines bear a vintage designation?

Because the American consumer has been conditioned to pay homage to French vintages. An aura of romance, glamour, and ultra-sophistication has surrounded the promotion of French wines in this country. Out of this has evolved a veritable vintage cult.

144

Does the French government rate the wines of each vintage?

No. The judging is done by individual wine brokers, shippers, importers, and trade associations.

145

What sort of rating codes is used for French vintages?

A numerical code or an expository code. The former employs numbers ranging from a low of two to a high of seven. The latter presents an ascending scale as follows: below average; fair; average; above average; great; very great.

146

Are French vintage ratings always in agreement?

No. While diametrically opposite judgments are impossible, shades of opinion do enter the picture. French wine authorities are trained and skilled. The task of assessing a given vintage, however, involves personal, subjective reactions, rather than scientific measurements.

147

Are top-rated French vintages commercially exploited?

Most assuredly. A well-publicized banner vintage evokes snob appeal among Francophile wine buffs. As with any commodity, when emotional undercurrents motivate the purchase, the consumer price skyrockets. It is par for the course for a "great" or "very great" year to command an extra three to seven dollars per bottle. In cases of very limited output, a surcharge of ten to fifteen dollars is not unheard of.

148

What is the key determinant of vintage quality?

The combination of rainfall, temperature and sunshine during the four to six weeks before the grape harvest. In most countries the interplay of these elements is fairly consistent from year to year.

149

Is the vintage of each French bottling rated individually?

No. All the reds and all the whites of a given district are lumped together under a single group rating. This blanket, or umbrella, judgment is one of the strongest objections to French vintage ratings.

150

What is a delimited European area?

A European viticultural area that has been awarded the exclusive legal right to certain specific type designations. Sherry, for instance, may not be so labeled unless it was produced within a clearly defined area of Spain. There is no such thing as Italian, French, or German Sherry.

151

How much wine does France produce?
Almost a billion cases a year.

152

How many acres of vines are under cultivation in France?
More than three million acres.

153

What kinds of wines are predominant in France?
Dry reds, rosés, and dry and semi-dry whites.

154

What are the two key premium-wine regions of France?
Bordeaux and Burgundy. Bordeaux is in the western part of the country near the Garonne and Dordogne rivers. Burgundy is in eastern France near the Swiss border.

155

What is meant by appellation contrôlée?
Appellation contrôlée is French for "name controlled." The term symbolizes a guarantee by the French government that the geography or origin shown on the label is authentic and that the wine has been made in accordance with a maximum yield per acre and from only specified grape varieties.

156

Does the appellation contrôlée *code apply to all of France?*
No . It applies only to Bordeaux, Burgundy, and some contiguous districts.

157

What is an inner appellation?

A specific district, village, or vineyard within Bordeaux or Burgundy.

158

Should an appellation-contrôlée *label be construed as a guarantee of quality?*

Not in an absolute sense. The major warranty set forth is that the identification of the wine is truthful and that fundamental standards of production have been met.

159

What is vin ordinaire?

The term means "ordinary wine." *Vin ordinaire* refers to the inexpensive, everyday kind of wine consumed by French civil servants, laborers, factory workers, artisans, tradesmen, and other Frenchmen of modest means.

160

What is vin du pays?

The young, fresh wine that abounds in the French countryside and rural hinterlands. *Vin du pays* is intended primarily for local consumption.

161

What are vin rouge *and* vin blanc?

Red *vin ordinaire* and white *vin ordinaire.*

162

What is a grand vin *French wine?*

The phrase has no official status. Its appearance on a French label is as inane as "special selection" on an American label.

163

What is a barrique?

A wooden wine barrel that many smaller Bordeaux châteaux use for storage and aging. A *barrique* holds 55 gallons of wine. Four *barriques* make up a *tonneau*, the liquid bulk measure of the Bordeaux wine industry. Bulk Bordeaux wine is bought and sold in *tonneau* units.

164

What is a chai?

The storage and aging room of a Bordeaux château.

165

What is a hectare?

A plot of French vineyard ground measuring 2½ acres.

166

What is a cuvée?

A French term that applies to a unit of wine earmarked: (1) for separate identification—as a numbered bulk purchase to show the particular source; or (2) for special use—as a lot set aside for blending, special handling, aging, processing, etc.

167

What is a côte?

A French vineyard situated on a slope or rolling hill. Wine made from grapes grown in such terrain is often labeled *"côte," "côteau," "côtes,"* or *"côteaux."*

168

What is a vigneron?

A French grape grower, vineyard master, or harvest superintendent.

169

What is négociant?

A French wine broker who "negotiates" a bottling or puts the package together, so to speak. He may contract for the harvest, purchase wine in bulk, arrange for vinification and bottling, and handle the distribution of the finished product.

170

What is a shipper?

A European wine exporter. The shipper may either buy wine in bulk and market the bottling under a trade name or act as a sales agent for one or more vintners.

171

What is a monopole French wine?

A blended bottling marketed under a shipper's exclusive trademark or monopoly.

172

What is a domaine, *or* clos?

A French vineyard parcel. A *domaine* may be an entity in itself, as a vineyard under single ownership, or one of a series of connecting plots that make up a vineyard entity. Whatever ground a grower owns is his *domaine*. The terms originated in the Burgundy region of France. In medieval times a *clos* was a vineyard property that was enclosed, or fenced in.

173

What is a château?

A French vineyard, especially a rather small vineyard situated in the Bordeaux region.

174

What is a registered château?

A Bordeaux vineyard, with an identity and a pedigree of its own, that cultivates premium grapes and has complete wine-production facilities. The word *château* may be freely adopted by a *négociant* or shipper in naming a wine. The name of a registered château, however, may be used only in connection with its own harvest or production. There are almost three thousand individually registered and recognized chateaux in Bordeaux.

175

What is a mis en bouteille au château *French wine?*

One that was vinified and bottled at the site of the harvest. The phrase stands for "château bottled."

176

What do the words mis en bouteille dans nos caves *stand for on a French wine label?*

Actually, nothing. A *cave* is the storage cellar and/or bottling department of a French wine house.

177

What is chaptalization?

The French practice of adding a few drops of sugar syrup to grape juice undergoing fermentation. This is a perfectly legitimate practice. Occasionally, an inadequate number of sunny days during the ripening season may leave the grapes a little short on natural sugar concentration. The liquid may ferment out at slightly less than the required alcohol content. Chaptalization is an accepted way of solving this problem.

178

What is pourriture noble?

The French term for "noble rot" or "noble mold," the bacterial coating that forms on the skins of certain grapes left on the vines beyond the normal harvesting date.

179

What is botrytis cinerea?

The scientific name for the fungus that causes "noble mold." This fungus seems to be compatible only with over-ripe green and yellow grapes. The fungus covers but does not lacerate the skins. The pulp is therefore spared from damaging exposure to air. As the grape withers the sugar concentration builds up, while the acidity and water content are reduced. When the grapes are pressed, the interplay of low water, low acid, and high sugar results in a liquid that is very low in quantity but extremely high in quality.

Curiously, *Botrytis cinerea* is attracted almost exclusively to French and German vines.

180

What are the principal grape varieties of Bordeaux?

Cabernet Sauvignon, Cabernet Franc, Merlot, Malbec, Petit Verdot (red wines); Sémillon and Sauvignon Blanc (white wines).

181

What is a cru?

A very good growth (crop). In French wine parlance the word refers to the supremely high quality of a vineyard's harvest from year to year through generations and even centuries.

182

What is a classified château?

A Bordeaux vineyard that has been officially accorded top *cru* standing. Of the region's 3,000 recognized châteaux, about 140 have been duly invested with this apex status. There is absolute agreement in the Bordeaux wine trade (and throughout the world) that these châteaux collectively produce the very best wines that the region has to offer. Within each Bordeaux district a separate classification has been established to identify these wines and set them apart from the rest of the output of the district.

183

How much of the wine from Bordeaux is from classified châteaux?

A fraction of 1 percent.

184

Are all classified châteaux equally ranked?

Some Bordeaux districts list all their classified properties under a single *cru* heading. Other districts set up as
many as five *cru* gradations as follows:

FIRST GROWTH:
premier cru, grand cru, premier grand cru

SECOND GROWTH:
deuxième cru

THIRD GROWTH:
troisième cru

FOURTH GROWTH:
quatrième cru

FIFTH GROWTH:
cinquième cru

185

Are cru numbers shown on the label?

No. A second, third, fourth, or fifth growth is identified
simply as a *"cru classé"* (classified growth) without further
delineation.

186

Do cru rankings change from year to year?

No. A *cru* evaluation is fixed and permanent. The
cardinal criterion—the natural composition of the soil—is
an enduring endowment.

187

Is a first growth five times better than a fifth growth?

No. To rate classified growths on a numerical basis would be akin to saying that a Cadillac Eldorado is two, three, four, or five times better than a Cadillac Coupe de Ville. It should be remembered that even a so-called fifth growth falls in the top 1 percent of all the wines produced in Bordeaux.

188

What is a cru bourgeois or cru exceptionnel?

A bottling from a non-classified Bordeaux château whose grape growth or grape crop is consistently excellent.

189

What is a petit château?

A lesser-known Bordeaux château whose wines are usually a cut above average.

190

What are the chief wine districts of the Bordeaux region?

Médoc, Saint-Emilion, Pomerol (red wines); Graves (reds and whites); and Sauternes (white wines).

191

How many first-growth Médoc wines are there?

Four. Château Latour, Château Lafite-Rothschild, Château Mouton-Rothschild (all in the commune, or parish, of Pauillac); and Château Margaux (in the commune of Margaux).

192

How much do these wines cost?

Prices start at about twelve dollars a bottle and run up to more than fifty dollars a bottle, depending on the shipper and the vintage.

193

How many other classified Médocs are there?

Fifty-six:

Château Batailley
Château Belgrave
Château Beychevelle
Château Boyd-Cantenac
Château Branaire-Ducru
Château Brane Cantenac
Château Calon-Ségur
Château Camensac
Château Cantemerle
Château Cantenac-Brown
Château Cos d'Estournel
Château Cos Labory
Château Clerc-Milon-Mondon
Château Croizer-Bages
Château Dauzac
Château Desmirail
Château d'Issan
Château Ducru-Beaucaillou
Château Duhart-Milon
Château Durfort-Vivens
Château du Tertre
Château Ferrière
Château Giscours

Château Grand-Puy-Ducasse
Château Grand-Puy-Lacoste
Château Gruaud-Larose
Château Haut-Bages-Libéral
Château Haut-Batailley
Château Kirwan
Château Lafon-Rochet
Château Lagrange
Château La Lagune
Château Langoa-Barton
Château Lascombes
Château La Tour-Carnet
Château Léoville-Barton
Château Léoville-Les-Cases
Château Léoville-Poyferre
Château Lynch-Bages
Château Lynch-Moussas
Château Malescot-Saint-Exupéry
Château Marquis-d'Alesme-Becker
Château Marquis-de-Terme
Château Montrose
Château Mouton-Baron-Philippe
Château Palmer
Château Pédesclaux
Château Pichon-Longueville
Château Pichon-Longueville-Lalande
Château Pontet-Canet
Château Pouget
Château Prieuré-Lichine
Château Rausan-Ségla
Château Rauzan-Gassies
Château Saint-Pierre
Château Talbot

194

When was the Médoc classification promulgated?

In 1855. The passing of time has upheld its validity beyond any shadow of a doubt.

195

What are the key Médoc parishes?

Of the sixty Médoc properties, fifty-seven lie in these six parishes: Pauillac (nineteen); Saint-Julien (eleven); Margaux (eleven); Cantenac-Margaux (eight); Saint-Estèphe (five); Saint-Laurent (three).

Ludon, Macau, and Arsac can lay claim to one each.

196

How much do these wines cost?

From six to twenty dollars a bottle.

197

How many crus bourgeois *or* crus exceptionel *Médocs have earned unimpeachable reputations?*

Thirty:

    Château Angludet
    Château Beau Site
    Château Bel-Air-Marquis-d'Aligre
    Château Capbern
    Château Chasse-Spleen
    Château Dutruch Grand Pujeaux
    Château Fourcas-Dupré
    Château Fourcas Hostein
    Château Glana
    Château Gloria
    Château Greysac

Château Haut Marbuzet
Château Labégorce
Château Lanessan
Château La Tour-de-Mons
Château Liversan
Château Loudenne
Château Marbuzet
Château Maucaillou
Château Meyney
Château Les Ormes de Pez
Château Paveil de Luze
Château Peyrabon
Château de Pez
Château Phélan-Ségur
Château Poujeaux-Theil
Château Siran
Château du Taillan
Château Tronquoy-Lalande
Château Verdignan

198

How much do these wines cost?
From four to eight dollars a bottle.

199

Is a Haut Médoc *better than a* Bas Médoc?
No. The words *"haut"* and *"bas"* mean "high" and "low." As used in connection with Médoc wines, they refer to the terrain of certain properties and have nothing to do with quality.

200

What are the two most prestigious wines of the Saint-Emilion district?

Château Ausone and Château Cheval Blanc. They are just as costly as the four Médoc first growths.

201

How many Saint-Emilion properties are ranked just a step under these two?

Ten:

> Château Beauséjour-Duffau-Lagarrosse
> Château Beauséjour-Fagouet
> Château Belair
> Château Canon
> Château Figeac
> Château Fourtet
> Château La Gaffelière (also called La Gaffelière-Naudes)
> Château Magdelaine
> Château Pavie
> Château Trottevieille

202

How many other Saint-Emilion growths have been classified?

Twenty-one:

> Château L'Angélus
> Château Balestard-la-Tonnelle
> Château Canon-la-Gaffelière
> Château Corbin
> Château Corbin-Michotte
> Château Curé-Bon

Château Dassault
Château Fonrocue
Château Grand-Corbin
Château la Clotte
Château des Jacobins
Château La Dominique
Château Larcis-Lucasse
Château La Tour-du-Pin-Figeac
Château Pavie-Macquin
Château Ripeau
Château Soutard
Château Tertre-Daugay
Château Trimoulet
Château Tropolong-Mondet
Château Villemaurine

203

Does Saint-Emilion follow the same classification pattern as Médoc?

No. There are only two categories—*premier grand cru classé* and *grand cru classé.*

204

When was the Saint-Emilion district classified?

Officially in 1955. The declaration, however, was purely academic, since the same vineyards had long been recognized as the district's leading properties.

205

Are there any noteworthy Saint-Emilion crus exceptionnels?

Yes, four: Château Curé-Bon-la-Madeleine; Château La Grâce-Dieu; Château Lapelletrie; Château Simard.

206

Does Saint-Emilion have any outstanding communes?

Yes, five: Saint Georges–Saint Emilion; Lussac–Saint-Emilion; Montagne–Saint-Emilion; Parsac–Saint-Emilion; Puisseguin–Saint-Emilion.

207

What is the price range of Saint-Emilion wines?

Excluding Château Ausone and Château Cheval Blanc, from four to fifteen dollars. Regional bottlings—those from anywhere within the district without any other appellation—are the most reasonable. In successive steps are village wines, *crus exceptionnels*, *grand crus*, and *premier grand crus*.

208

Is Pomerol a large viticultural area?

No. Pomerol's output is only about 15 percent that of Médoc or Saint-Julien.

209

Do most Pomerols bear a vineyard appellation?

Yes. There is very little regional Pomerol. About 90 percent of the wine of this district displays the name of a vineyard.

210

What is the most famous wine of Pomerol?

Château Pétrus, which retails for from fifteen to forty dollars a bottle.

What are some other well-known Pomerol properties?

Château Gazin, Château Lafleur, Château La Pointe, Château Nénin, Clos René, Château Petit-Village, Château Trotanoy, and Château Taillefer.

212

How much do these wines cost?

From eight to twelve dollars.

213

Has Pomerol ever been officially classified?

Not in any systematic or formal code. It is generally agreed that most of the registered châteaux in this relatively small district are of *cru* status. The several cited above are first-growth wines.

214

What is the most celebrated vineyard of the Graves district?

Château Haut-Brion.

215

How are Graves properties classified?

With the exception of Château Haut-Brion, Graves vineyards were officially judged in 1953. Château Haut-Brion had rightfully been accorded stellar honors in conjunction with the Médoc classifications of 1855.

Cru classifications were granted to fourteen other properties on an equal plane, without graduated rankings. Château Haut-Brion, of course, has always enjoyed a niche unto itself.

216

Which Graves vineyards have won cru *status?*

    Château Bouscat
    Château Carbonnieux
    Domaine de Chevalier
    Château Couhins
    Château de Fieuzal
    Château Haut-Bailly
    Château Kressman La Tour (also called La Tour-
      Martillac)
    Château La Mission-Haut-Brion
    Château La Tour-Haut-Brion
    Château Laville-Haut-Brion
    Château Malartic-Lagravière
    Château Olivier
    Château Pape Clément
    Château Smith-Haut-Lafitte

217

How expensive are cru classé *Graves wines?*

Twelve to fifty dollars for Château Haut-Brion. The others average six to fourteen dollars, with the exception of Château La Mission-Haut-Brion and Domaine de Chevalier, which are both pegged a few dollars higher.

218

Why is Graves said to be unique in Bordeaux viticulture?

Because it is the only district where classified châteaux vinify both red and white wines. The former are much more prevalent.

If a French label reads "Graves," with no other appellation, what sort of wine is in the bottle?

A three- to five-dollar dry or semi-dry white wine.

220

What kind of wine is the Sauternes district noted for?

Semi-dry whites of distinguished character. Tart or astringent wines are almost never seen in Sauternes because the native grapes are high in natural sugar and low in acid. A degree of residual sweetness is inevitable after fermentation. Sauternes wines may be enhanced by "noble mold."

221

What is the most honored wine of Sauternes?

Château d'Yquem. Prices start at twelve dollars a bottle and escalate to more than forty dollars.

222

What is the history of Sauternes classifications?

This district, like the Médoc, was classified in 1855. Château d'Yquem was at that time (and still is) one of the world's most prestigious vineyards and was assigned a *grand premier cru* classification of its own. Other outstanding Sauternes properties were classified as first and second growths. It has been said through the years that the line of demarcation between Sauternes first and second growths is largely academic.

223

How many cru classé *Sauternes are there?*

Twenty-three besides Château d'Yquem:

Château Broustet
Château Caillou
Château Climens
Château Coutet
Château D'Arche
Château Doisy-Daëne
Château Doisy-Védrines
Château Filhot
Château Guiraud
Château Haut-Peyraguey
Château Lafaurie-Peyraguey
Château Lamothe
Château La Tour-Blanche
Château de Malle
Château Myrat
Château Nairac
Château Rabaud-Promis
Château de Rayne-Vigneau
Château Rieussec
Château Romer
Château Sigalas-Rabaud
Château Suau
Château de Suduiraut

224

How does a Sauternes differ from a Haut Sauternes?

As a rule the latter is sweeter—how much sweeter depends upon the supplier. The wines of the Sauternes district, regular or *haut,* are the least dry of the entire Bordeaux region. Some Sauternes bottlings, in fact, have an aftertaste approaching that of a dessert wine.

225

Is there a difference between Sauternes and Barsac?

Not really. Barsac is a village within the district. The viticultural characteristics of Barsac are the same as those of the rest of the district.

226

What is the price range of Sauternes?

Regional bottlings and Barsacs are in the three-to-six-dollar category. Those from classified vineyards may run almost double that.

227

What is Sainte-Croix-du-Mont?

A district half the size of Sauternes, on the opposite bank of the Garonne River from Sauternes. If it were not for this small boundary line, Sainte-Croix-du-Mont would be treated as a subdivision of Sauternes. The soil conditions, weather conditions, and grape varieties are the same.

228

How do Sauternes and Sainte-Croix-du-Mont wines and prices compare?

A Sainte-Croix-du-Mont is the equal of a regional Sauternes bottling at one to two dollars less.

229

Why do some Bordeaux properties have similar names?

Because of the family ties of some of the original owners. A number of individual parcels were granted to or

acquired by brothers, nephews, cousins, and other members
of the same family circle. The family name, or parts
thereof, became attached to more than one château.

230

*Are most of the Bordeaux châteaux under single-family
ownership?*

Yes. Almost all are owned by one individual or one
family group. Multiple ownership, or joint participation by
individuals, each holding a piece of a vineyard, has never
been a Bordeaux tradition.

231

*How much wine does the average classified vineyard pro-
duce?*

Most produce less than twenty thousand cases annually. More than half have an output of less than ten thousand cases annually.

232

Do all classified Bordeaux producers do their own bottling?

Not all of them. Some consign the finished product
in bulk to one or more shippers who handle the packaging
and distribution of the bottling.

233

*Can the wine of a classified Bordeaux vineyard be counter-
feited or bootlegged?*

Absolutely not. A wine showing a vineyard appellation
is from that property and nowhere else. Not one drop of
wine from any other source may be introduced. Nor does it
matter whose name appears on the label as the shipper.
Even aside from the protection of an *appellation contrôlee,*

a run-of-the-mill wine could hardly masquerade as a great growth.

234

Are liberties even taken with the names of famous châteaux?

Yes. It is not unheard of for an unscrupulous *négociant* or shipper to market a bottling under a fictitious château name that sounds very much like the "real McCoy." The attempted deceit may be further compounded by showing a company address in the same locality. The giveaway, however, is the *appellation contrôlee.*

235

What is Entre-Deux-Mers?

A large district adjacent to Bordeaux. It is so named because it lies "between two seas" (rivers)—the Garonne and the Dordogne.

236

What is the output of Entre-Deux-Mers?

More than five million cases a year.

237

Does Entre-Deux-Mers boast any stellar vineyards?

No. The ten thousand or so acres under cultivation are equal. No one vineyard parcel has a loftier pedigree or heritage than any other.

238

What sort of wines come from Entre-Deux-Mers?

Light, pleasant, agreeable white table wines. There is no such thing as a red Entre-Deux-Mers bottling. The small quantity of red wine that is produced is labeled simply as Bordeaux Rouge.

239

What are the secondary districts of Bordeaux?

Blaye, Bourg, Cerons, Côtes de Bordeaux, Fronsac, Loupiac, Saint Macaire, Sainte Foy–Bordeaux, and Bergerac.

240

How are the wines from these districts characterized?

They may, of course, lack some of the finesse of some of the great Bordeaux wines, but they are, in their own right, truly sound, honest, well-made wines. These wines, as well as those from Entre-Deux-Mers, are usually priced from $2.50 to $4.00 a bottle. Many wine buffs whose palates have been trained on good Bordeaux bottlings have found to their pleasant surprise that a Blaye, Fronsac, or other secondary Bordeaux can be an enjoyable experience at a modest price.

241

What is Monbazillac?

An exceptionally fine semi-dry white wine from Bergerac.

242

What is Bordelaise?

A group name for any wine from the Bordeaux region.

243

What is Claret?

A group name for any red Bordeaux wine.

Is the Burgundy region as productive as the Bordeaux region?

No. Burgundy produces only about 40 percent as much wine as Bordeaux.

245

Do Burgundy classifications parallel Bordeaux classifications?

No. Burgundy is much more village oriented. Although some individual properties have gained international recognition, viticultural emphasis has centered around a number of key villages, communes, and parishes.

Burgundy has never been classified in the same official *cru* context as Bordeaux. Its great vineyards and villages have become famous through continued excellence from generation to generation.

246

How many subdivisions make up the Burgundy region?

Seven. From north to south, they are Chablis, Côte de Nuits, Côte de Beaune, Chalonnais, Mâcon, Beaujolais, and the Rhône Valley.

247

What kind of wine is associated with the Chablis district?

The wine named for this district is decidedly dry white made from Pinot Chardonnay grapes.

248

How is Chablis laid out geographically?

Although it is spoken of as a district, Chablis is more accurately a sprawling rural complex consisting of the town proper, scores of surrounding vineyards, and miles of outlying properties.

249

Which Chablis vineyards are worthy of individual mention?

> Les Beugnon
> Les Blanchots
> Les Bougros
> Les Clos
> Les Fôrets
> Les Fourchame
> Les Grenouilles
> Les Preuses
> Les Valmur
> Les Vaulorent
> Les Vaudésir

These bottlings are truly of *grand cru* caliber and may be so labeled.

250

What is Petit Chablis?

A wine vinified from grapes harvested in the outer reaches or peripheral sections of the Chablis district.

251

What is the price range of Chablis wines?

Less than four dollars for a Petit Chablis, from four to six dollars for a district bottling, and from six to nine dollars for a *grand cru*.

How many important villages or communes are there in Côte de Nuits?

Eight. From north to south they are:

Fixin
Gevrey-Chambertin
Morey-Saint-Denis
Chambolle-Musigny
Vougeot
Flagey-Echezeaux
Vosne-Romanée
Nuits-Saint-Georges

Which of these villages have fewer than five famous vineyards?

Vougeot: Clos de Vougeot
Flagey-Echezeaux: Echezeaux; Grands-Echezeaux
Chambolle-Musigny: Les Amoureuses; Bonnes Mares
(a portion thereof); Les Charmes;
Musigny
Fixin: Les Arvelets; Clos du Chapitre; Les Hervelets;
Clos de la Perrière
Clos Napoleon is sometimes included in Fixin listings.

What are some other well-known vineyards of Côte de Nuits?

By villages as follows:

Gevrey-Chambertin:

Les Cazetiers
Chambertin

Chambertin-Clos-de Bèze
Chapelle-Chambertin
Charmes-Chambertin
Combe-au-Moine
Griotte-Chambertin
Latricières-Chambertin
Mazoyeres-Chambertin
Mazys-Chambertin
Ruchottes-Chambertin
Clos-Saint-Jacques
Varoilles

Morey-Saint-Denis:

Bonnes Mares (a portion thereof)
Clos Bussière
Clos des Lambrays
Clos de la Roche
Clos Saint-Denis
Clos de Tart

Nuits-Saint-Georges:

Aux Boudots
Les Cailles
Clos des Corvées
Les Didiers
Aux Perdrix
Les Porrets
Les Pruliers
La Richemone
Clos de la Maréchale
Les Saint-Georges
Aux Thorey
Les Vaucrains

Vosne-Romanée:

Les Beaumonts
Aux Brûlées
Les Gaudichots
La Grande Rue
Les Malconsorts
Clos des Réas
Richebourg
La Romanée
Romanée-Conti
Romanée-Saint-Vivant
Les Suchots
La Tâche

255

What type of wine is associated with Côte de Nuits?

Côte de Nuits production is devoted almost entirely to dry reds.

256

Are there any noteworthy Côte de Nuits dry white wines?

Yes—Musigny Blanc, Clos Blanc de Vougeot, and Nuits-Saint-Georges Les Perrières.

257

Is there any rosé wine of Côte de Nuits origin?

Yes. Marsannay, a settlement just beyond the northern boundary but viticulturally included in the district, has created a lovely rosé from Pinot Noir grapes.

258

Which Côte de Nuits village has the smallest output?

Fixin, which bottles only 2 to 3 percent of the dis
trict's wines.

259

Which Côte de Nuits village has the largest output?

Nuits-Saint-Georges, which accounts for nearly one-
third of the district's production.

260

*Does all Nuits-Saint-Georges wine come from the village
proper?*

No. Some territorial leeway has been granted. The
neighboring settlement of Prémeaux, for instance, is per-
mitted to bottle its wine as Nuits-Saint-Georges. Prémeaux
is an excellent viticultural settlement. The use of the more
familiar appellation is a courtesy that has evolved through
the years.

261

*What are the foremost wine-producing villages of Côte de
Beaune?*

Dry red:

Pernand-Verglesses
Savigny
Pommard
Volnay
Monthélie
Auxey-Duresses
Santennay

Dry white:

Meursault
Puligney-Montrachet

Dry red and dry white:

Aloxe-Corton
Beaune
Chassagne-Montrachet

262

Which Côte de Beaune vineyards are famous for dry red wines?

By villages as follows:

Pernand- Verglesses:

Ile-des-Verglesses

Aloxe-Corton:

Le Corton
Corton Bressandes
Corton Clos du Roi
Corton Maréchaudes
Corton Les Meix
Corton Renardes

Savigny:

Les Dominode
Les Jarrons
Les Lavières
Les Marconnets
Les Vergelesses

Beaune:

    Les Avaux
    Les Bressandes
    Clos du Roi
    Les Fèves
    Les Grèves
    Les Marconnets
    Les Clos des Mouches
    Les Cent Vignes

Pommard:

    Les Clos Blanc
    Les Chaponnières
    Les Epenots
    Les Pézerolles
    La Platière
    Les Rugiens

Volnay:

    Les Caillerets
    Les Champans
    Le Clos des Chênes
    Clos des Ducs
    Les Fremiets
    Santenots

Monthelie:

    Les Champs Fuillots

Auxey-Duresses:

    Les Duresses
    Clos du Val

Chassagne-Montrachet:

Clos de la Boudriotte
Les Caillerets
La Maltroie
Morgeot
Clos Saint-Jean

Santenay:

Gravières
Clos Tavannes

263

Which Côte de Beaune vineyards are famous for dry white wines?

By villages as follows:

Aloxe-Corton:

Charlemagne
Corton Charlemagne

Beaune:

Les Clos des Mouches

Meursault:

Blagny
Charmes
Les Genevrières
La Goutte d'Or
Les Perrières
Poruzot
Santenots

Puligny-Montrachet:

Montrachet
Bâtard-Montrachet
Bienvenue-Bâtard-Montrachet
Chevalier-Montrachet
Les Caillerts
Le Champ Canet
Les Chaluneaux
Clavoillon
Les Combettes
Les Folatières
Les Pucelles
Les Referts

Chassagne-Montrachet:

Montrachet
Bâtard-Montrachet
Criots-Bâtard-Montrachet
Les Caillerets
Les Chenevottes
Morgeot
Les Ruchottes

264

Do some Côte de Beaune vineyards lie in two villages?

Yes. The groupings above show a handful of parcels that encroach upon the territory of adjacent villages. The acreage involved is limited, and the viticultural hierachy is in no way affected.

265

Is there a common name for Côte de Nuits and Côte de Beaune?

Yes. The contiguous districts are collectively known as Côte d'Or, or Slope of Gold—*Slope* because of the hilly topography; *Gold* because of the summer sun and the fall foliage.

266

What proportion of Burgundy's wines are from Côte d'Or?

Scarcely one-eighth, about 90 percent of which is dry red.

267

What is Côte d'Or's largest vineyard?

Clos de Vougeout. Its 125 acres are subdivided among one hundred growers.

268

Are most Côte d'Or properties under individual ownership?

No. Almost all of the one hundred or so prime properties are apportioned into numerous plots. The *domaine,* or tract, of each grower seldom exceeds an acre or two.

269

How did multiple vineyard control come about?

The properties were originally held by religious organizations and the aristocracy. Both groups were forced to relinquish their rights and interests during the French Revolution. The tracts were subsequently broken up and conveyed to hundreds of Burgundy farmers.

270

Does a multiply owned Côte d'Or vineyard operate under a uniform code?

No. Each grower prunes, tends, and cultivates on his own, without inspection or supervision.

271

Does such individualism lower the quality of the harvest?

On the contrary it tends to bring about the very best that each *domaine* and each grower is capable of offering. Côte d'Or growers and vintners are motivated by an abiding sense of tradition and pride. Moreover, the care and effort that go into choice crops are handsomely rewarded in the marketplace.

272

What is a tête de cuvée *Côte d'Or vineyard?*

In trade circles those properties which constitute the cream of the harvest are lauded as "the head of the *cuvée*." The phrase may be used in labeling a prestigious Côte de Nuits or Côte de Beaune bottling.

273

What is the Hospices de Beaune?

A charitable hospital that has assembled more than one hundred acres of prized Beaune vineyards through gifts of inheritance. In the late fall the Hospices stages a harvest and wine auction that attracts buyers from international markets. The profit helps the institution carry on its charitable work.

274

How are Hospices de Beaune tracts individually noted?

The memory of the benefactor takes precedence over the site of the plot or the name of the successful bidder. Each *cuvée*—three dozen in all—is a perpetual tribute to the donor.

275

Which Hospices de Beaune cuvées are the most celebrated?

Cuvée Blondeau
Cuvée Charlotte Dumay
Cuvée Gauvin
Cuvée Guigone de Salins
Cuvée Nicolas Rollin
Cuvée Docteur Peste

Guigone de Salins and Nicolas Rollin were married to one another and were instrumental in founding the hospital five centuries ago.

276

What does the word villages *denote on a Côte d'Or label?*

The countryside of Côte d'Or is dotted with hamlets and settlements that make fairly good wines but are too diminutive to have appelations of their own. Wine from these sources may be sold as Côte de Nuits–Villages, Côte de Beaune–Villages, or Nuits-Saint-Georges–Villages.

277

What are the predominant Côte d'Or grape varieties?

Pinot Noir (red wines) and Pinot Chardonnay (white wines).

278

What is a champ?

A rural field or narrow strip of Côte d'Or vineyard ground.

279

What is the price range of Côte d'Or wines?

From four to ten dollars for those with a village name and from six to twenty-five dollars for vineyard appellations.

280

Why is Côte d'Or often described as the Heart of Burgundy?

Because the finest and costliest bottlings of the whole region are from Côte de Nuit and Côte de Beaune vineyards.

281

What is the most popular wine of Chalonnais?

Mercurey, a dry red made from Pinot Noir grapes.

282

What are the outstanding wine villages of Chalonnais?

Besides Mercurey there are Rully, Givry, Montagny, and Chalon-sur-Saône.

283

Does Chalonnais have any inner appellations?

Not in the same framework as the key areas of Côte d'Or. A Chalonnais label may show a village appellation, but the wine is commercially viewed as a good regional bottling.

284

Are there any inner appellations for the red wines of Mâcon?

No. Mâcon reds are regional bottlings. There are no geographical subdivisions or single properties of international repute.

285

What kind of wine is Mâcon?

A wine so labeled is usually a dry red made from Gamay (Gamay Beaujolais) grapes.

286

What is the Mâcon district's claim to viticultural fame?

Pouilly-Fuissé, a charming dry white wine.

287

Which Mâcon villages are associated with Pouilly-Fuissé?

Pouilly and Fuissé are both wine communes. The nearby villages of Solutré, Chaintré and Vergisson are also top rated.

288

How much does Pouilly-Fuissé cost?

Between five and ten dollars.

289

What is Pouilly-Vinzelles?

A dry white wine from the Mâcon settlement of Vinzelles. Pouilly-Vinzelles is a rung below Pouilly-Fuissé on the viticultural ladder.

290

What is the largest wine district of Burgundy?

Beaujolais. At least 30 percent of all the wines broadly classified as Burgundy are of Beaujolais origin.

291

Which grape variety is closely identified with Beaujolais?

The Gamay—so closely, in fact, that the Gamay grape has become known as Gamay Beaujolais.

292

What kind of wine is Beaujolais?

A mild, light-bodied dry red with a pronounced fruity, flowery bouquet.

293

How popular is Beaujolais in the United States?

Extremely. Beaujolais is one of the most called-for French wines in the United States. Its mass appeal is quite understandable. Beaujolais is a fundamental, uncomplicated wine that can be savored without homage to the intricacies of French viticulture.

294

What are the leading village of the Beaujolais district?

Brouilly
Côte de Brouilly
Chénas
Chiroubles
Fleurie
Juliénas
Morgon

Moulin-à-Vent
Saint-Amour

295

What is the relationship between Brouilly and Côte de Brouilly?

They are neighboring villages in the desirable northern section of Beaujolais. Côte de Brouilly is the site of a string of hillside vineyards. The vineyards of the two villages are among the prettiest landscape scenes in all of Beaujolais.

296

What is a Beaujolais-Villages wine?

A bottling from a village in central Beaujolais. Although these twenty-five or thirty villages have no name value of their own, their wines are better than average.

297

Is there any real difference between a Beaujolais and a Beaujolais-Supérieur?

Hardly. The original criteria, alcohol content and yield per acre, have been outdated. In all practical aspects the two bottlings are the same.

298

What is Beaujolais Nouveau?

Nouveau means "new" or "of the current year." A 1975 Beaujolais would be called Beaujolais nouveau until the appearance of the 1976 bottling, whereupon the 1976 bottling would be known as Beaujolais nouveau.

299
What is Beaujolais Primeur?

A Beaujolais bottled on or about November 15, barely two months after the grapes have been picked. At the time of bottling, Beaujolais primeur is delightfully refreshing. Because the vatting period is so short the wine is perishable. A Beaujolais primeur will begin to "turn" by the following winter.

300

What is the life expectancy of other Beaujolais wines?

Beaujolais is a young, vivacious wine that cries out to be consumed within three years. An older Beaujolais may be on the dull, vapid side.

301

How extensive is the Rhône Valley?

It is quite spread out. The district stretches for 130 miles, from below the Lyons junction of the Saône and Rhône rivers, to the approach to the seaport of Marseilles.

302

What is Côtes du Rhône?

A group classification for the lesser wines of the district, most of which are dry reds.

303

What the the principal grape varieties of the Rhône Valley?

Carignan, Clairette, Counoise, Grenache, Marsanne, Mourvedre, Muscardin, Picpoule, Roussanne, Syrah, Terret Noir, Ugni Blanc, Viognier.

304

What is Chusclan?

A Rhône village noted for rather good rosé wines.

305

What is Gigondas?

A Rhône village whose wines are superior to those labeled simply as Côtes du Rhône.

306

What is Côte Rotie?

A superb red Rhône wine. Syrah is the chief grape variety. A moderate amount of Viognier, a white grape, is blended with Syrah for a beautifully smooth, well-balanced wine.

307

What is Château Grillet?

A classic Rhône white wine ranked among the world's finest whites. The vineyard itself is scarcely bigger than an American athletic field.

308

What is the difference between Hermitage and Crozes-Hermitage?

Hermitage is a northern Rhône village center known for excellent dry reds and dry whites. The wines of Crozes-Hermitage, which takes in the surrounding environs, are of a slightly lower character.

309

What is Tavel?

A Rhône village that has gained an international reputation for lovely rosé wines. The grape variety is Grenache, which thrives in Tavel as in few other places in the world.

310

What is Lirac?

A village near Tavel. Lirac rosés are also vinified from Grenache grapes and are sometimes spoken of as cousins of Tavel wines.

311

What is the most famous wine of the Rhône Valley?

Châteauneuf-du-Pape, which translates as "the new château of the pope." This viticultural complex lies near Avignon, in the southern tier of the Rhône Valley.

312

What is the ecclesiastical background of Châteauneuf-du-Pape?

The French Pope Clement V moved the official residence from Rome to Avignon in the fourteenth century. A summer estate, Châteauneuf-du-Pape, was simultaneously built ten miles away. Vineyard acreage flourished here until the partial destruction of the vacation retreat in the sixteenth century. The reclamation and recultivation of the land in the nineteenth century precipitated the growth of the viticultural industry for miles around.

313

What kind of wine is Châteauneuf-du-Pape?

A full-bodied red table wine. A small quantity of white Châteauneuf-du-Pape is also marketed, but hardly enough to be of any real commercial importance.

314

Is Châteauneuf-du-Pape made from a single grape variety?

No. The vineyards of Avignon are heavily diversified. A dozen varieties are under cultivation, any and all of which may be utilized in vinifying Châteauneuf-du-Pape. The better bottlings are made from the juices of six to eight different varieties.

315

Could Châteauneuf-du-Pape be made from a single variety?

No. What distinguishes a Châteauneuf-du-Pape from an ordinary Côtes du Rhône is the blissful marriage of different kinds of grapes, each lending its own attributes to the finished product. No single variety of the Rhône Valley could possibly yield a wine akin to this.

316

Does Châteauneuf-du-Pape contain more alcohol than Beaujolais?

Yes. Beaujolais is 9 to 11 percent alcohol by volume. By law, Châteauneuf-du-Pape must contain a minimum of 12½ percent alcohol. The oppressive heat of the Rhône valley produces grapes that give off a high concentration of alcohol during fermentation.

317

Does Châteauneuf-du-Pape have a longer life span than Beaujolais?

Yes. A well-made Châteauneuf-du-Pape will keep twice as long as a Beaujolais.

318

How do Beaujolais and Rhône Valley prices compare?

Beaujolais wines are three to five dollars. The nine village appellations are the highest priced.

Rhone wines fall into the following pattern:

$ 2.00–3.50:
  Côtes du Rhone
3.00–5.00:
  Chusclan
  Gigondas
  Lirac
  Tavel
4.00–6.00:
  Hermitage
  Crozes-Hermitage
  Côte Rotie
5.00–9.00:
  Châteauneuf-du-Pape
15.00–20.00:
  Château Grillet

319

Is the Rhône Valley always treated as a Burgundy district?

No. It depends on how hair splitting one wishes to be in discussing French wines. Some Francophiles would be reluctant to include any area beyond Mâcon or Beaujolais. Châteauneuf-du-Pape is mass marketed in the United

States as a Burgundy, however, and the Rhône valley has become fully accepted in the wine industry as part of Burgundy.

320

What is Bourgogne?

A group name for Burgundy wines.

321

What is Bourgogne Aligoté?

A white Burgundy vinified from Aligote instead of Pinot Chardonnay grapes. This variety lacks some of the delicacy and finesse of the Chardonnay.

322

What is Bourgogne-Passe-Tout-Grains?

A red wine from Côte de Nuits or Côte de Beaune vinified from a combination of Pinot Noir and Gamay grapes. The Gamay juices makes for a wine that is a bit lighter in body than most Côte de Nuits and Côte de Beaune wines. It is sometimes called *Bourgogne-Passe-Tous-Grains*.

323

Where is the Loire River?

It flows for 625 miles in central and western France.

324

What kinds of wines come from the Loire Valley?

An array of pleasant, reasonably priced reds, whites, and rosés.

325

Which grape varieties are widely planted along the banks of the Loire?

Cabernet Franc, Muscadet, Sauvignon Blanc, Chenin Blanc, Groslot, and Chasselas.

326

Which Loire River reds have achieved recognition?

Bourgueil, Champigny, Chinon, and Saint Nicolas. All are Cabernet Franc wines.

327

Is there a kinship between Muscadet and Muscatel?

Absolutely none. The similarity of nomenclature is an unfortunate coincidence. Muscadet grapes are indigenous to the Loire department of Brittany. Muscadet is a delightful, light, dry white wine.

328

What is the viticultural heritage of muscadet?

Muscadet vines were first planted in central and northern Burgundy with disappointing results. About five hundred years ago roots were transferred to the banks of the Loire River, where the interplay of ideal soil and weather engendered optimum wine grapes.

329

Is Muscadet a bountiful crop?

Decidedly. The Muscadet harvest approaches that of Beaujolais.

330

What is Sèvre-et-Maine?

An area near Nantes, in Brittany. The primary muscadet bottlings come from here.

331

What is Lie Muscadet?

Lie is French for lees, the fruit suspensions that accumulate in the barrel while the liquid is fermenting and aging. A *Lie Muscadet* is one that is drawn from the barrel through the fruit suspensions. The wine is bottled young and has a light-bodied freshness.

332

Could Muscadet be called a varietal wine?

Yes. In fact, Muscadet is one of the few French wines that could accurately be spoken of as a genuine varietal.

333

Which Loire white wines are made from Sauvignon Blanc grapes?

Quincy, Sancerre, and Pouilly-Fumé. These are a bit fuller-bodied than Muscadet.

334

Which Loire white wines are made from Chenin Blanc grapes?

Vouvray and Saumur. Chenin Blanc is the region's sturdiest variety. In its Loire habitat it acquires a chemical balance that endows Vouvray and Saumur with a remarkable life span of up to ten years.

335

What are some of the lesser-known Loire whites?

Bonnezeaux, Côteaux de l'Aubance, Côteaux du Layon, Côteaux de la Loire, Montlouis, and Quarts de Chaume. These fairly good wines will become better known in the American market thanks to the promotional efforts of importers and distributors.

336

What is Anjou Rosé?

A semi-dry Rosé. Anjou Rosé, or Rosé d'Anjou, is named after a district of France that includes Angers, a city on the Loire River. Anjou Rosé is vinified from Groslot grapes.

337

What is Anjou Rosé Cabernet?

A Loire rosé made from Cabernet Franc grapes. Cabernet Franc creates a more refined, more flavorful rosé than the Groslot.

338

What is Pouilly-sur-Loire?

A Loire river village. The wine so designated is a dry white prepared from Chasselas grapes. There is no connection between the two Pouilly bottlings of the Loire Valley —sur-Loire and Fumé—and the Pouilly-Fuissé of Mâcon.

339

Does Pouilly-Fumé have a smoky overtone?

No, although *fumé* does mean "smoke" in French. For reasons obscured by conflicting tales and antiquity the Sauvignon Blanc grape has been tagged as *blanc fumé* —"white smoke"—in Loire folklore.

340

Where is the Provence district?

On the Mediterranean Sea. It stretches for 110 miles between Marseilles and Nice.

341

What class do Provence wines fit into?

The reds and whites are dependable, everyday wines. The rosés are more sophisticated.

342

How are Provence wines labeled?

As Côtes de Provence, Rosé de Provence, Vin de Provence, or Bouquet de Provence.

343

Do any Provence villages warrant special attention?

Yes—Bandol for reds and rosés and Cassis for whites.

344

Does the village of Cassis have any link with Cassis liqueur?

No. The liqueur is a sugary, currant-based concoction from northern Burgundy.

345

What is Hérault?

A large *vin ordinaire* district in southern France.

346

What is the Midi?

An extensive region in southern France. The Midi stretches east and west from Italy to Spain and north and south from the Rhône valley to the Mediterranean. Provence and Hérault are Midi subdivisions.

347

What percentage of France's wine production is from the Midi?

More than 35 percent. The Midi eclipses Bordeaux and Burgundy combined in total gallonage.

348

What are the key areas of the Midi?

Provence, Cahors, Corbières, Costières du Gard, Languedoc, Minervois, and Côtes de Ventoux.

349

What is the caliber of Midi wines?

About 90 percent is *vin ordinaire*; 10 percent can be equated with some of the good wines of Bordeaux and Burgundy.

350

What is a French country wine?

A better-than-average Midi wine. The term is fairly new and was devised to popularize Midi wines in the United States.

351

What is a French V.D.Q.S. wine?

The initials stand for *"vins délimités de qualité supérieure."* The top wines of the Midi are so labeled.

352

How much do Midi V.D.Q.S. wines cost?

Seldom more than three dollars. Because of steep Bordeaux and Burgundy price hikes in recent years, increased attention has been focused on V.D.Q.S. wines. Many of them are excellent buys in today's market.

353

What is Alicante Bouschet?

A grape variety indigenous to the Midi region. Its juice has a crimson tint, a rare phenomenon. Alicante Bouschet lacks sufficient depth to stand on its own but is fairly well suited for blending.

354

What is Folle Blanche?

A white grape processed as a base for French brandy. By contrast, Folle Blanche grapes harvested in California are vinified into a varietal wine. It is a curious sidelight that some varieties fare better away from their place of birth.

355

What is Charente?

A rather thin, insipid white wine from the Cognac district in western France. Its primary use is for distillation into Cognac.

356

Do other French wines sacrifice some of their identity in the vinification process?

Yes. Colombard, Mataro, Mondeuse, and Mourestel are grape varieties that have little identification with a finished product but do play a role in blending and processing.

357

What is the Jura district?

A small area in eastern France. Jura whites, reds, and rosés are shipped to the United States.

358

Do any Jura wines stand above the field?

Yes—Arbois and Jurancon.

359

What is Jura's proudest viticultural accomplishment?

Château Chalon, a mild white wine that has sensory nuances of a dry sherry. The fermented liquid is aged three to five years in an undersized wooden vessel. A minute flow of air is allowed to seep into the barrel creating a "blanket" of oxidized yeast cells. Painstaking care must be exercised to ensure that oxidation heightens, rather than diminishes, the delicacy of the liquid.

360

What is the viticultural name for this unique wine?

Vin Jaune. Needless to say, *Vin Jaune* can be turned out only in nominal quantities. It will "keep" in the bottle for more than fifty years.

361

What is the retail price of Château Chalon?

From twelve to fifteen dollars a bottle.

362

What is Crépy

A dry white wine vinified in the French Alps from Chasselas grapes.

363

Are Bordeaux and Burgundy wine bottles similar?

No. A Bordeaux bottle is cylindrical up to a point several inches from the top, where it is indented or rounded off on either side to join with a columnar neck. A Burgundy bottle is broad at the base and slopes gradually to a narrow neck.

364

Is there a traditional container for French rosé wines?

No. Bottle shapes and designs are limited only by the supplier's creative imagination. French rosé packages may be slender, stubby, angular, contoured, round, rectangular. They may be molded as decorative carafes, urns, decanters, jugs, crocks.

365

Where is the Alsace (Alsace-Lorraine) region of France?

Along the French-German corridor formed by the Rhône River and the Vosges Mountains.

366

How many Alsatian grape varieties are there?

Three—Riesling, Sylvaner, and Traminer.

367

Are there any off-shoots of these varieties?

Yes. Gewürztraminer is a Traminer derivative. Traminer vines sporadically sprout clusters with a somewhat pungent, spicy accent. These vines are set aside for special vinification. *Gewürz* is German for "spicy."

368

Is Gewürztraminer ranked above Traminer?

Yes. Gewürztraminer is the king of Alsatian wines.

369

Is the Alsatian harvest bountiful?

Yes—bountiful enough for eight to ten million cases annually.

370

What is the viticultural history of Alsace?

Vines were first planted here during the era of the Roman Empire and have bloomed ever since. The viticultural sanctity of Alsace has been preserved through centuries of heated French-German contention. Geographically, Alsace has been part of France since 1918 except for Germany's World War II occupation. Alsatian grapes, however, have always been governed by German nomenclature.

371

Is Alsace viticulturally diversified?

No. Its output consists wholly of dry white varietals.

372

How much do Alsatian wines cost?

Riesling, Sylvaner, and Traminer cost $2.50 to $3.50. Gewürztraminer costs a dollar more.

373

Do Alsatian and German viticulture overlap?

In a narrow context. Riesling, Sylvaner, and Traminer are common to both countries. But unlike Germany, Alsace is characterized by uniformity from border to border, with no districts, villages or vineyards ranking higher than others.

374

Do vines bloom throughout Germany?

No. The weather of much of Germany is too severe.

375

How many vineyards are there in Germany?

Reliable estimates put the figure at seventy-five thousand. The vast majority encompass one to three acres. Perhaps one out of a hundred is of fifteen acres or more. With few exceptions, these larger tracts are held by old-line families or by the government.

376

Which grape variety produces the finest German wines?

Riesling is the undisputed cock of the walk. Sylvaner and Traminer growths in certain sections of Germany have acquitted themselves beautifully. Müller-Thurgau, a Riesling-Sylvaner hybrid, has made rapid strides in recent years.

377

How much alcohol do German vines contain?

Germans prefer robust beer but mild wine. Few German wines come anywhere near 14 percent by volume. Most contain from 8 to 11 percent.

378

Into which two wine regions is Germany divided?

The Rhine and the Moselle. All the grapes of Germany are grown near these two rivers and their tributaries, whose fresh water provides a temperate zone of tremendous fertility.

379

How is the Rhine region viticulturally divided?

Into Rheinhessen (Middle Rhine), Rheinpfalz (Palatinate), and Rheingau. The first two are huge districts that produce 50 to 60 percent of all German wine. Rheingau vineyards occupy only about 7,000 acres between Weisbaden and Rudesheim. From these vineyards come some of Germany's most magnificent bottlings.

380

Do both whites and reds come from the Rhine region?

Yes. The whites, however, predominate by a twenty-to-one ratio.

381

Which Rhine municipalities are associated with red wines?

Assmannshausen (Rheingau), Ingelheim (Rheinhessen) and Baden, Durkheim and Wurttemberg (Palatinate).

The grape varieties are Burgunder, a Pinot Noir descendant, and a Portuguese transplant called Portugieser. The German red wine most often seen in the United States is Durkheimer Feuerberg. For some curious chemical reason German reds, especially those from the Palatinate, seem to have a headiness which belies their comparatively low alcoholic content.

382

Has any Rhine type become a household word in the United States?

Yes. Liebfraumilch. "Lieb" is "love" or "loving." "Frau" signifies womanhood or feminine gender. "Milch" is "milk" or, in this case, "wine." Translated with some degree of license, Liebfraumilch is the "milk or wine of the Beloved or Blessed Mother." It is thought that the religious twist may be a throwback to the church vineyards of centuries ago. Liebfraumilch is a blended wine which may come from anywhere within the Rhine region. Liebfraumilch is the leading type of imported white wine in the United States. Liebfraumilch is a prototype wine. If you are familiar with the taste characteristics of Liebfraumilch, you have a reasonable working knowledge of what most Rhine wines are all about. The soft, light, gentle, mild quality is a family trait.

383

What is Niersteiner?

A wine from the Rheinhessen village of Nierstein. Niersteiner and Liebfraumilch are quite similar in style.

384

Is Niersteiner Domtal a special bottling?

No. "Domtal" may be translated as "a steeple in the valley." The reference is said to stem from medieval church vineyards which were situated in Rhine valleys. Niersteiner and Niersteiner Domtal are identical wines.

385

What other Rhine types are marketed in the United States?

Oppenheimer (Rheinhessen) and Rudesheimer and Johannisberger (both Rheingau). The "er" ending means "of" or "from." Generally speaking, these are village wines blended from Sylvaner or Riesling grapes.

386

How much do these five wines cost?

Generally, from two to four dollars. A few will bring a dollar more.

387

Are Oppenheimer Goldberg and Oppenheimer Krötenbrunnen regional or vineyard bottlings?

Regional. The compound name has to do with wine merchants, rather than growers. These Oppenheimer wines are in wide distribution in the United States.

388

What is the Moselle counterpart of Liebfraumilch?

Moselblümchen—the "bloom," or "flower," of the Moselle. This blended wine can be vinified from grapes harvested anywhere along the Moselle river. It is sometimes spelled Moselbluemchen.

389

Which Moselle village blends have been well received in the United States?

Bernkasteler, Piesporter, and Zeltinger. It is permissible to join the village and the grape variety to form a compound name such as Bernkasteler Riesling, Piesporter Riesling, or Zeltinger Riesling.

390

What is Zeller Schwarze Katz?

"Black cat" wine from the Moselle town of Zell. Legend has it that there was once a Zell vintner who had a black cat with a penchant for sniffing barrels of wine. The cat is supposed to have purred at the most fragrant barrels and hissed at the least fragrant.

391

What is Kröver (Crover) Nacktarsch?

"Bare buttocks" wine from the Moselle town of Kröv (Cröv). According to legend a mischievous tyke snuck into a Kröv wine cellar while the proprietor was away. He proceeded to sample the fermented grape juice of several barrels, whereupon he sank into a dazed sleep. When the cellar master returned he surveyed the scene and quickly deduced what had happened. He roused the youngster, put him over his knee, and applied an open palm to his bare bottom.

392

Are Rhine and Moselle prototypes similar in style?

Up to a point. Both are young, light-bodied, soft, semi-dry wines. Moselles, however, seem to exhibit a group tendency toward a more fruity bouquet. This difference is caused by the more extensive cultivation of Riesling grapes in the Moselle region.

393

What is spritz?

The slight tingle or faint prickly sensation that is captured in a number of German bottlings.

394

Which Rheinhessen vineyards are equated with the cream of the harvest?

Niersteiner Rehbach
Niersteiner Hipping
Niersteiner Heiligenbaum
Niersteiner Orbel
Nackenheimer Rothenberg
Nackenheimer Engelsberg
Nackenheimer Fenchelberg
Nackenheimer Fritzenhöll
Oppenheimer Kreuz
Oppenheimer Steig
Oppenheimer Daubhaus
Oppenheimer Sackträger
Binger Büdesheimer Scharlachberg
Binger Kempter Rheinberg
Binger Rochusberg
Bodenheimer Hoch

395

What are the most esteemed vineyards of Rheinpfalz?

Forster Kirchenstück
Forster Jesuitengarten

Forster Ungenheuer
Forster Freundstück
Deidesheimer Grainhubel
Deidesheimer Herrgottsacker
Deidesheimer Hohenmorgen
Deidesheimer Kieselberg
Ruppertsberger Spiess
Ruppertsberger Nussbien
Ruppertsberger Gaisbohl
Wachenheimer Gerumpel
Wachenheimer Bachel
Wachenheimer Bohlig
Wachenheimer Altenburg

396

Which Rheingau vineyards are world famous?

Schloss Johannisberg
Schloss Vollrads
Steinberg
Marcobrunn
Hochheimer Domdechaney
Hochheimer Rauchloch
Hochheimer Holle
Hochheimer Raaber
Rauenthaler Baiken
Rauenthaler Wülfen
Rauenthaler Gehrn
Raunethaler Herberg
Rauenthaler Wieshell
Rauenthaler Ofaffenberg
Rauenthaler Langenstück
Erbacher Steinmorgen
Erbacher Brühl
Hattenheimer Nussbrunnen

Hattenheimer Engelsmannberg
Winkeler Hasensprung
Winkeler Jesuitengarten
Winkeler Dachsberg
Johannisberger Klaus
Johannisberger Kochsberg
Johannisberger Hölle
Johannisberger Erntebringer
Rüdesheimer Berg Rottland
Rüdesheimer Berg Lay
Rüdesheimer Berg Bronnen
Rüdesheimer Berg Schlossberg
Rüdesheimer Wilgert
Rüdesheimer Klosterkiesel
Eltviller Sonnenberg
Eltviller Grauer Stein
Eltviller Langenstück
Eltviller Taubenberg
Kiedricher Gräfenberg
Kiedricher Sandgrub
Hallgartener Schönhell
Hallgartener Deutelsberg
Hallgartener Mehrhölzchen
Geisenheimer Rothenberg
Geisenheimer Mauerchen
Ostricher Lehnchen
Ostricher Eiserberg
Ostricher Magdalengarten
Wallufer Walkenberg
Wallufer Mittelberg

397
Which Rhine district has the choicest individual properties?
Rheingau beyond any doubt. In land dimensions

Rheingau is dwarfed by Rheinhessen and Rheinpfalz, but it has a larger number of prime vineyards than its two compatriots combined. Vineyard for vineyard, Rheingau is said to be one of the two or three top white wine districts on the face of the earth.

398

If Rheingau grows the same grape variety as Rheinhessen and Rheinpfalz, why are its wines superior?

For two reasons. First, Rheingau's vineyards are planted on waterfront slopes that face south. The direct rays of the sun, and those reflected from the water, play on the vines at desirable angles. Second, at this point in its course the Rhine becomes a tranquil lake instead of a massive river. The warm, moist vapors that rise from the water circulate benevolently through the vineyards.

399

Where is Franconia?

Midway between Frankfurt and Würzburg on the Main River, a tributary of the Rhine. This is a small area whose wines are drier and more full-bodied than most Rhines and Moselles.

400

Which are Franconia's most notable vineyards?

Würzburger Stein
Würzburger Aussere Leiste
Würzburger Innere Leiste
Würzburger Neuberg
Eschendorfer Lump
Eschendorfer Eulengrube
Eschendorfer Kirchberg

Iphofer Julius Echter Berg
Iphofer Kronsberg
Randersackerer Pfülben
Randersackerer Spielberg
Randersackerer Teufelskeller
Casteller Schlossberg
Homburger Kallmuth
Randersackerer Hohburg

401

Which of these vineyards is most familiar to American consumers?

Würzburger Stein (or Stein by itself) has been so heavily publicized here that Franconian wines are frequently labeled simply as Steinwein. Wurzburger Stein's four hundred acres make it Germany's biggest vineyard. The property is state owned.

402

Which vineyards are the pride of the Moselle region?

Bernkasteler Doktor
Bernkasteler Badstube
Bernkasteler Rosenberg
Bernkasteler Lay
Graacher Himmelreich
Graacher Josephshof
Graacher Domprobst
Piesporter Goldtröpfchen
Piesporter Schubertslay
Piesporter Taubengarten
Piesporter Falkenberg
Wehlener Sonnenuhr

Wehlener Lay
Wehlener Nonnenberg
Wehlener Klosterlay
Zeltinger Sonnenuhr
Zeltinger Schlossberg
Zeltinger Rotlay
Zeltinger Himmelreich
Brauneberger Juffer
Brauneberger Falkenberg
Erdener Treppchen
Erdener Pralat
Urziger Würzgarten
Urziger Kranklay
Trittenheimer Laurentiusberg
Trittenheimer Altarchen
Neumagener Engelgrube
Neumagener Rosengartchen
Dhroner Hofberg
Dhroner Grosswingert
Wintricher Ohligsberg
Wintricher Grosser Herrgott
Lieser Niederberg
Lieser Schlossberg

403

Do any charitable institutions own Moselle property?

Yes—Bischöfliches Konvikt (the Bishop's Convent),
Bischöfliches Priesterseminar (the Bishop's Ministerial
Seminary), Vereinigte Hospitien (United Hospital), and
Frederich Wilhelm Gymnasium (Frederich Wilhelm
School of Higher Learning). The name of the institution,
rather than the vineyard, is shown on the label.

404

Where is the Nahe Valley?

The Nahe is a Rhine tributary that flows south from Rheingau and parallel and close to the Moselle. Despite its narrow confines, the Nahe Valley brings to market a sizable inventory of excellent wines.

405

How many Nahe wine villages are there?

Eight—Laubenheim, Winzenheim, Rüdesheim, Bad Munster A Stein, Norheim, Wald Bockelheim, Schloss Bockelheilm, and Neiderhausen.

406

Do the names of any of these villages call for further elaboration?

Two of them do. Schloss Bockelheim sounds like a vineyard property but is not. The Rüdesheim of the Nahe Valley and the Rüdesheim of Rheingau are unrelated municipalities, like Newark, New Jersey, and Newark, Delaware.

407

What is Rüdesheimer Rosengarten?

A blended Nahe wine marketed under a town-bottler name. Careful reading of the label discloses that the package is neither an estate nor a Rheingau bottling.

408

What are the key Nahe Valley vineyards?

Kreuznacher Hinkelstein
Kreuznacher Kahlenberg
Kreuznacher Mönchberg

Kreunznacher St. Martin
Niederhauser Hermannshöle
Niederhauser Hermannsberg
Niederhauser Pfingstweide
Norheimer Kafels
Norheimer Hinterfels
Norheimer Dellchen
Schloss Böckelheimer Kupfergrube
Schloss Böckelheimer Felsenberg
Schloss Böckelheimer Mühlberg
Roxheimer Birkenberg

409

What is the tie between the Saar Valley and the Ruwer Valley?

The Saar and the Ruwer are parallel Moselle tributaries that form a pair of viticulturally kindred districts. Wines from either district that have no village or vineyard inscription are packaged as Saar-Ruwer or Moselle-Saar-Ruwer.

410

Which Saar villages are wine centers?

Scharzhof, Wiltingen, Ockfen, Ayl, Konz, Oberemmel, Wawern, Ganzem, Nittel, Winche, Ringen, Niederleuken, and Saarburg.

411

What are the principal vineyards of the Saar Valley?

Scharzhofberg
Wiltingener Braune Kupp
Wiltingener Scharzberg
Wiltingener Klosterberg

Wiltenginer Gottesfuss
Wiltinginer Kupp
Ockfener Bockstein
Ockfener Geisberg
Ockfener Herrenberg
Ockfener Heppenstein
Ayler Kupp
Ayler Herrenberg
Ayler Neuberg
Oberemmeler Altenberg
Oberemmeler Hütte
Oberemmeler Scharzberg
Kanzemer Sonnenberg
Niedermenniger Euchariusberg
Wawerner Herrenberg

412

How many Ruwer villages are wine centers?

Five—Maximin, Kasel, Eitelsbach, Waldrach, and
Grunhaus.

413

What are the leading vineyards of the Ruwer Valley?

Maximin Grünhauser Herrenberg
Maximin Grünhauser Bruderberg
Kaseler Niesgen
Kaseler Hitzlay
Kaseler Kohlenberg
Kaseler Taubenberg
Eitelsbacher Karthäuserhofberg
Eitelsbacher Marienholz
Waldracher Schloss Marienlay
Waldracher Ehrenberg

113

414

What is a Spätlese *German wine?*

"Spät" is German for "late." "Lese" refers to the picking of the vines. A Spätlese wine is one made from grapes harvested days or weeks after the bulk of the crop has been laid in. This additional span intensifies ripeness if the elements of nature are friendly. There is a calculated risk on the part of the grower. Excessive rainfall, harsh temperatures or inadequate sunshine can puncture the dream of a prize yield.

415

What is an Auslese *German wine?*

Auslese means "picked out." An *auslese* wine is one that was made from late-picked grapes from a designated plot within the vineyard. "Aus" describes the practice of singling out the choicest section of the vineyard for late-picking.

416

What is a Beerenauslese *German wine?*

Beeren is German for "berries" or "grapes." The *Auslese* bunches are examined berry by berry. Those berries or grapes which are extra ripe are removed from the clusters and pressed separately.

417

What is a Trockenbeerenauslese *German wine?*

Trocken is German for "dry." The reference in this context is to grapes that have a withered, dried-out appearance. *Trockenbeerenauslese* symbolizes the absolute ultimate in berry-by-berry selection of the cream of the late-picked harvest. A wine so designated is made from grapes that are individually hand picked, that are the ripest of the ripe, that have the highest concentration of natural sugar, and that display the greatest evidence of "noble mold."

418

What is Edelfäule?

The German expression for "noble mold."

419

How sweet are German "lese" wines?

A *Spätlese* may have only a suggestion of sweetness. An *Auslese* is somewhat more pronounced. *Beerenauslese* and *Trockenbeerenauslese,* like French Sauternes, are decidedly sweet.

420

May All German Wines Be Made From Late-Picked Grapes?

No. The official German code excludes Liebfraumilch and Moselblumchen. The theory is that the geography of many of these bottlings is too general or too non-definitive. This rule was enacted in 1974, so that some Liebfraumilch Spätlese and Moselblumchen Spätlese may still be in retail inventories in the United States.

421

What is Eiswein?

"Ice wine." As a rule, frost is detrimental to vines. The exception may occur in German vineyards when a gentle frost follows several days of sunshine. If the grapes have completely ripened, the white crystalline coating will lock in the natural sugar content of the fruit.

422

What is Tafelwein?

"Tafel" is German for "table." A German blended wine whose geography is of a broad, general nature is officially designated as a Tafelwein.

423

What is a Qualitätswein?

A German wine from a delimited area, a specific village or an individual vineyard.

424

What is a Qualitätswein mit Pradikat?

"Pradikat" means "special attribute" in German. The "pradikat" in this case has to do with "lese" grapes. A Qualitätswein of at least Spätlese caliber is officially identified as a Qualitästwein mit Pradikat.

425

What is a Cabinet (Kabinett) *German wine?*

A *Qualitätswein mit Pradikat* drawn from a special lot signifying the cream of the harvest.

426

What is a Fass?

The barrel number, as shown on the label, from which a particular lot of Rhine wine was bottled.

427

What is a Fuder?

The barrel number, as shown on the label, from which a particular lot of Moselle wine was bottled.

428

Which German terms convey the idea of a proprietary interest in a vineyard or winery?

Lage, Schloss, Weingut, and *Weinkeller.*

429

Which German terms express the idea of estate bottling?

Originalabfüllung, Aus dem lesegut, Aus eigenem lesegut, and *Erzeugerabfüllung.*

430

What is a Staatsweingüter *bottling?*

A Rheingau wine from a federally controlled vineyard. The government owns more than three hundred acres of vineyard property—more than any other grower in Rheingau.

431

What is a gezuckerter *or* verbesserter *German wine?*

Zucker is "sugar"; *bessern* is "to make better" or "to improve." When grapes ripen too early in the season or are denied their quota of sunshine, the extract may be a little deficient in natural sugar. It is permissible to add a small quantity of sugared water to the fermenting liquid.

432

What is a German Natur *wine* (Naturrein)?

One fermented from grape juice completely free of any *zucker.* Implicit therein is a warranty that the grapes ripened to full perfection.

433

What is Edelwein?

Edel is German for "noble" or "high bred." This inscription is sometimes seen on a bottling a vinter deems to be a shining example of his craftsmanship.

434

Is a German vineyard notation an absolute guarantee that the wine is not a regional or village bottling?

Not always. Some vineyards create their wines from a mix of their own grapes and those purchased from village growers. This practice is perfectly legitimate, with no intent to deceive. The purpose is to assure consistent uniformity. The finished product may indeed be superior to some estate bottlings but an *Originalabfüllung* notation would, of course, be prohibited. In such instances it is understood that the vineyard is the shipper that assembled the package.

435

Which recognized vineyards follow this practice?

Bernkasteler Braunes
Graacher Münzlay
Piesporter Michelsberg
Niersteiner Fritzenhölle
Hochheimer Daubhaus
Johannisberger Erntebringer
Eltviller Steinmacher
Urziger Schwarzlay

436
What is Hock?

A class name for Rhine wines. The term is becoming an anachronism in the United States but is still current British terminology. Hock is an Anglicized abbreviation of Hochheim, the German city from which boatloads of Rhine wine were once shipped to England.

437
Are there any German Rosé wines?

No. Germany's red grape varieties are too demanding for this purpose.

438
What is Maywine?

A Rhine wine flavored with woodruff, a semi-pungent herb. Wine festivals used to be staged in Rhine villages in May, with competitive events for the best entries. Wines infused with botanicals were perennial crowd pleasers.

439
What is the utility grape species of the Moselle region?

Elbing (also called Elbling). This is a prolific, plump grape that matures early with a minimum of attention. On its own, Elbing ferments into a young, fresh country wine that is consumed locally. It is also serviceable for blending and for vinification into sparkling wine.

440
Are Rhine and Moselle wine bottles of like design and color?

Both regions use tall, tapered containers. Rhines are bottled in brown glass; Moselles in green.

441

Are Franconian wines bottled in Rhine and Moselle containers?

No. Franconia has adopted the *bocksbeutel,* which is short, round, and bulbous.

442

What is the surcharge for Spätlese *and* Auslese *wines?*

A *Spätlese* is worth from 50 cents to $1.50 extra per bottle; an *Auslese* from $2.00 to $3.00 additional.

443

What percentage of the German harvest is a beeren *growth?*

A fraction of 1 percent.

444

How expensive are beeren *wines?*

Very. They are among the world's costliest white wines. *Beerenauslese* carries a fifteen- to twenty-dollar tag. *Trockenbeerenauslese* can run two to three times as much.

445

How expensive is Eiswein?

Roughly in the same category as *Beerenauslese.*

446

What is the price structure of German vineyard wines?

The spectrum is broad. About 75 percent of the German wines of specific vineyard origin are priced at less than six dollars a bottle. The top 25 percent range from six to fifteen dollars, with gradations of one dollar or less straight up the line.

447

If there were an international hall of fame for vineyards, which German properties would be elected to membership?

An impartial panel of professionals would find no fault with the following list:

Würzburger Stein	Franconia
Ockfener Bockstein	Saar valley
Scharzhofberg	Saar valley
Maximin Grünhauser Herrenberg	Ruwer valley
Wehlener Sonnenuhr	Moselle
Graacher Himmelreich	Moselle
Piesporter Goldtröpfchen	Moselle
Erdener Treppchen	Moselle
Brauenberger Juffer	Moselle
Forster Jesuitengarten	Rheinpfalz
Oppenheimer Sacktrager	Rheinhessen
Schloss Johannisberg	Rheingau
Eitelsberger Karthauserhofberg	Ruwer valley
Schloss Vollrads	Rheingau
Steinberg	Rheingau
Marcobrunn	Rheingau
Rudesheimer Berg Rottland	Rheingau
Niersteiner Orbel	Rheinhessen
Bernkasteler Doktor	Moselle

448

How long will German wines keep in the bottle?

Regional and village wines will start to lose some of their refreshing light-heartedness after three or four years. Prime vineyard bottlings will retain the essence of their liveliness and finesse for up to twice as long. *Beeren* wines are virtually indestructible.

449

Can a family name take top billing on a German wine label?

Yes, especially when the property owner's family tree has noble roots. Some of the more prominent unions are

Matuschka-Grieffenclau. . . . Schloss Vollrads
Dr. H. Thanisch. . . . . Bernkasteler Doktor
Egon Müller. . . . . Scharzhofberg
J. J. Prüm. . . . . .Graacher Himmelreich
and Wehlener
Sonnenuhr

450

Do German designations such as Blue Nun, Madonna, Glockenspiel, Madrigal, and Wedding Veil denote any special attributes?

These are exclusive trademarks that certain shippers have taken for their Rhine and Moselle prototypes. When a wine merchant feels that his Liebfraumilch or Zeller Schwarze Katz stands above the crowd he may market it as a proprietary brand.

451

Do the German adjectives feine *and* feinste *have any viticultural importance?*

Not any more. The German government declared such adjectives to be too vague, under a new labeling code implemented during the 1971–72 season.

452

Is a natural tingle in wine a uniquely German phenomenon?

No. The spritz that is gently embodied in some German wines is also present in some of the wines of Portugal,

Italy, the United States, and France (a Vouvray specialty). In the United States and France the effect of malolactic fermentation is called *pétillance*.

453

Is there a legal limit to the natural effervescence that may be caused by malolactic fermentation?

Yes. U.S. excise tax schedules fix the maximum at 227 milligrams per 100 milliliters of carbon dioxide. A more gaseous liquid would lose its still-wine tax status.

454

Is artificial carbonation permissible?

Yes. Compressed gas may be pumped into the beverage, as in the manufacture of soda. Carbonated wines are subject to a federal excise levy of $2.40 per gallon.

455

Can champagne be created through malolactic fermentation?

No. Malolatic fermentation is too passive.

456

What gives champagne its sparkle?

Secondary fermentation, a process that enables carbon dioxide to be trapped in the storage tank or in the bottle itself.

457

How is secondary fermentation activated?

After the still wine has come to rest a mixture of syrup (sugar and water) and yeast cells is added. The sugar-yeast aditive restimulates a churning of the liquid.

458

Does secondary fermentation increase alcohol content?

No. The liquid has already been invested with its full potency. Further fermentation would be of no avail.

459

Does secondary fermentation take place in the same vat as primary fermentation?

No. Primary fermentation has taken place in an open vessel. The wine is now either transferred in bulk to a closed tank or actually bottled. The sugar and yeast are then introduced, whereupon the bulk tank is sealed or the bottles are crowned with a removable clamp.

460

Why must secondary fermentation take place in airtight surroundings?

To prevent the newly formed carbon dioxide from escaping into the atmosphere. The object of secondary fermentation is to *capture* the gas, which will render the wine bubbly.

461

How long does it take for a still wine to become sparkling wine?

Secondary fermentation takes from two to four months. The beverage is then aged for from three months to three years.

462

What are the technical terms for secondary tank fermentation?

Bulk process or Charmat Process. When sparkling wine is created in this fashion it must be so labeled.

463

What are the technical terms for bottle-incited secondary fermentation?

Méthode Champenoise or *tirage.* A sparkling wine so processed may be labeled as "naturally fermented in the bottle."

464

What is the distinction between "naturally fermented" and "fermented in the bottle" Champagne?

The former phrase is employed to enhance the consumer image of a bulk, or charmat, Champagne. All Champagne, to be sure, is naturally fermented. But only a *tirage,* or *Méthode Champenoise,* product can be marketed as "naturally fermented in the bottle."

465

What is riddling?

The individual racking of bottles during the transformation from still wine to champagne. Riddling racks may be designed as floor bins, A-frames, or honeycomb nests. The essential requisite is that each bottle have a slot or "pigeon hole" of its own in which it can be laid horizontally, slanted downward, and rotated.

466

Is bottle fermentation a tedious process?

Yes. The yeast and sugar throw off a sediment, which must be withdrawn from the bottle. Over a span of months each bottle is given a gentle twist once a day so that the solidified crust is ultimately lodged in the neck. There is no mechanical way to move the sugar-yeast sediment from the bottom of the bottle to the top.

467

How is sediment removed in bulk fermentation?

Mechanically. The sugar-yeast residue can be siphoned or pumped from the tank.

468

What is disgorgement?

The removal of sediment from the bottle after secondary fermentation and aging. The neck is inserted into frigid brine, thereby holding the residue in frozen suspension. The closure is then unclamped. The carbon-dioxide pressure in the bottle forcibly ejects the sediment.

469

What is dosage?

The replacement of the ounce or more of liquid lost in disgorgement with a syrup solution. After disgorgement and *dosage* the bottles are quickly transferred from the riddling racks to the bottling line, where the package is permanently sealed.

470

Why is a champagne bottle thicker than a still-wine bottle?

Because the internal pressure—six times that of the outside atmosphere—could cause regular gauge glass to burst.

471

Is Champagne a blended wine?

Yes. It would be difficult to achieve an ideal balance of taste components or to maintain consistency from lot to lot without skillful blending.

472

Is bottle fermentation feasible for every size Champagne package?

No. The jeroboam (and often the magnum) is too unwieldy for riddling. The split is too diminutive for individual handling. These sizes are filled with Champagne bottle fermented in 25.6-ounce containers.

473

How many levels of Champagne dryness are there?

Three—brut, extra dry, and sec. Brut is the driest; extra dry is semi-dry; sec is on the sweet side. There are no universal or official criteria, so one brand of brut may be drier than another, etc.

474

What determines whether a Champagne is brut, extra dry, or sec?

The proportion of sugar in the syrup utilized in *dosage*.

475

What is Crémant?

A French sparkling wine whose effervescence is softer than that of Champagne.

476

What is Sparkling Burgundy?

A sparkling red wine. The color comes about through *cuvaison*.

477

Can champagne be bottled throughout France?

No. The use of the name is legally restricted to the department, or district, of Champagne, which lies to the north of Chablis. Nor can the name be used anywhere else on the Continent.

478

What are the key subdivisions of the Champagne district?

Avize, Ay, Cramant (no connection with crémant sparkling wine), Epernay, and Reims.

479

Does the Champagne district package any still wines?

Yes, but for decades the exportation of still wines from the Champagne district has been forbidden. The ban has just been lifted and small shipments are on their way here. Two still wines from Champagne are slated for distribution in the United States. One is a Chablis-like bottling known as Saran Nature, which takes its name from Chateau Saran near Epernay. The other is a dry red called Bouzy Rouge after the village of Bouzy.

480

Which grape varieties are legally sanctioned in the Champagne district?

Pinot Noir and Pinot Chardonnay. The standard *cuvée* is made from four units of Pinot Noir to one unit of Pinot Chardonnay.

481

What is Blanc de Blanc Champagne?

Champagne processed wholly from white grapes. French Blanc de Blanc must be made only from Pinot Chardonnay grapes.

482

Does the Champagne district have its own vineyard rating code?

Yes. The yardstick of excellence is the chalkiness of the soil. Champagne properties are duly authenticated on a five-to-ten scale. Upwards of half the grapes harvested in the department are of nine or ten rank.

483

Is a vintage French Champagne superior to a non-vintage?

The consensus of professional opinion shies away from an affirmative position. The wisdom of formulating a *cuvée* from the grapes of a single year is open to debate unless the harvest is spectacular. It is widely maintained that two consecutive harvests are necessary for a harmonious balance.

484

What percentage of the champagne consumed in the United States is imported from France?

Less than 6 percent.

485

Is New York State champagne better than California champagne?

It depends on whom you talk to and what you are talking about. Both states produce mediocre as well as great sparkling wines. The best of either state would please the most discriminating palate.

486

What is the basic difference between New York State and California cuvées?

New York State Champagne is largely a Catawba derivative (together with some Delaware). California bulk champagne is vinified from almost any grapes at hand. Premium California bottlings contain vinifera juices including some Pinot Noir and Pinot Chardonnay pressings.

487

Is the New York–California cuvée disparity a critical element?

Not really. The base wine, regardless of its composition, must be of an acceptable grade. What ultimately winds up in the bottle, however, is controlled by the integrity and expertise of the supplier. Neither state has a monopoly on that score.

488

How much does Champagne cost?

From two to eight dollars for American Champagne, from seven to twenty-five dollars for French Champagne.

489

How long will sparkling wine keep in the bottle?

A top-notch sparkling wine, American or French, could conceivably retain its bouquet, flavor, and effervescence for up to ten years if the closure stays hermetically sealed. It should be stressed that even a pinpoint infiltration of air will turn the beverage flat and sour in a few months.

490

Is a plastic cap as airtight as a cork?

Yes, possibly even more so. It is also cheaper and easier to insert at the winery.

491

What is the major objection to a plastic Champagne cap?

It has less prestige and snob appeal than a cork.

492

Does Champagne improve in the bottle?

No. The wine has already been brought to its apex before permanent sealing.

493

How important is the shape of the glass into which effervescent wine is poured?

Very. The carbon dioxide bubbles will fizzle out rather quickly in the shallow, wide-mouthed sort of glass used in numerous catering establishments. A tapered or tulip-shaped glass with a constricted mouth will trap the bubbles and agitate a lively upward movement. A hollow-stemmed glass will create a continuing geyser-like effect. Unfortunately this type of glass is difficult to wash thoroughly and is outlawed for commercial service in some states.

494

Why is the neck of a Champagne bottle covered with foil?

The equivalent of two or three teaspoonfuls of liquid can bubble away between *dosage* and permanent sealing. The foil wrapping is intended to overcome the visual handicap of an occasional short fill.

495

What is the purpose of the wiring under the neck foil?

It is a safeguard against the possibility that the internal pressure of the carbon dioxide might uncap the bottle.

496

To what extent should effervescent wines be chilled?

Divergent opinions have long centered around this issue. There are those who hold that an hour of refrigeration or immersion in a bucket of ice cubes is sufficient. Such superficial treatment may cause the wine to gush out with a frothy splash and to fall flat in a wink. Others contend that a crackling or sparkling beverage should be chilled in the same way as beer or soda. A temperature of thirty-five to forty-five degrees will precipitate tiny, longer-lasting bubbles. Effervescent wines can be safely kept under refrigeration for months.

497

What are the most urgent precautions to observe in opening a bottle of sparkling wine?

There are three. First, handle the bottle gently. Unnecessary shaking or pulling can cause the liquid to surge forth explosively. Second, avoid direct contact between the warm hand and the cold bottle. It is a good idea to wrap the bottle in a napkin or towel. Third, point the neck of the bottle away from persons or objects within close range.

498

What are the safest ways to open a bottle of sparkling wine?

There are two alternatives after slow and careful removal of the neck foil and wiring. Hold the fingers of one hand on the closure and rotate the bottle in a series of short, gentle turns or hold the bottle in one hand and with the other push the closure upward with a minimum of force.

499

Can a partially consumed bottle of Champagne be hermetically resealed?

It is difficult to reinsert a cork without allowing a stream of air to seep in. A plastic cap, though, can be effectively reset into the neck of the bottle. The remaining liquid will stay in satisfactory condition for two or three days.

500

How many calories in an ounce of effervescent wine?

About thirty.

501

Is a crakling wine as effervescent as a sparkling wine?

No. The carbon dioxide pressure is decidedly more subdued.

502

Do all crackling wines undergo secondary fermentation?

No. A crackling wine may be artificially carbonated.

503

Which kind of wine is enhanced most by a crackling effervescence?

Rosés seem to take on more visual and sensory appeal than other types.

504

What is the excise tax on a fifth of sparkling wine?

The national average is about $1. The federal rate is $3.40 a gallon, or 68 cents a fifth. Each state tacks on its own fractional supplementary levy.

505

Does the type of sparkling wine affect the tax rate?

No. Carbon dioxide is the common denominator. The retail price, the country of origin, the method of production, etc., are of no consequence.

506

Is the federal excise tax the same for crackling wines as for sparkling wines?

No. The former are assessed at $2.40 a gallon instead of $3.40. Most states, however, tax crackling wines and sparkling wines at the same rate.

507

Can flavoring agents be added to sparkling wines?

Yes. Several years ago there was a frenzied trend toward fruit-flavored bottlings. Some are still in distribution, but none has been dramatically successful.

508

What is Cold Duck?

A mixture of Champagne and Sparkling Burgundy. This concoction took the United States by storm in the late sixties and for two or three years accounted for one-half of all the sparkling-wine sales here. The Cold Duck trend has since waned.

509

Where does the name Cold Duck *come from?*

From the German *kalte ende,* or "cold ends"—the few unconsumed drops that inevitably remain in a bottle of sparkling wine. In German restaurants it was customary for bartenders and kitchen help to salvage the *kalte ende* of the day's wine business as an ingredient for their own private "pinch of this, dash of that" improvisations. Somewhere along the line the *ende* became colloquialized into *ente*—German for "duck."

510

What is Sekt?

German sparkling wine.

511

What is Espumosa?

Spanish sparkling wine.

135

512

What is Aguja?

A Spanish wine with a prickly sensation upon the tongue. The name is derived from the Spanish word for "needle." Although Aguja is actually a still wine, it goes through malolactic fermentation, which triggers a buildup of carbon dioxide.

513

What is Doux?

A French sparkling wine that has been double or triple *dosaged* to compensate for inadequacies in the base liquid. A doux sparkling wine is much sweeter than a sec.

514

What is Mousseux?

Any French effervescent wine bottled anywhere in the country except the department of Champagne.

515

What is Spumante?

Italian sparkling wine.

516

How far back does Italy's viticultural heritage go?

Wine has been an everyday Italian household staple for nearly three thousand years. From the outset, wine drinking has transcended social and economic barriers. The enjoyment of wine has always been shared equally by Italians in all walks of life, from the humblest peasant to the lordliest aristocrat.

517

How do the Italians look upon wine?

In a basic, mundane, down-to-earth way. The esoteric snobbery, mystique, worshipful reverence, and super-sophistication that pervade some aspects of French winedom are alien to Italian thinking.

518

Which sections of Italy are best suited for grape cultivation?

No single area can be spotlighted. Italy's soil and weather are so favorable that vineyards are to be found everywhere. Grapes flourish in every nook and cranny of Italy.

519

Does Italy's grape tonnage surpass that of France?

The two nations have long been engaged in a see-saw race for quantity leadership. Proportionately, Italy's output is more remarkable, since this country occupies less than two-thirds as much territory as France.

520

What percentage of the world's wine is either French or Italian?

Roughly 45 percent in any given year—an astounding figure, but France and Italy are astounding wine countries.

521

How many different wines does Italy produce?

Somewhere between five hundred and one thousand. Every Italian city, town, village, and hamlet lays proprietary

claim to a host of bottlings of individualized nomenclature.

522

Are all these Italian wines exported to the United States?

No. Only a few dozen Italian wines are marketed here.

523

Are grapes grown in conjunction with other Italian crops?

Sometimes. For generations grapes, grains, fruits, and vegetables were intermingled in some settlements. This practice is fast waning as Italy seeks to update and upgrade its viticultural image.

524

What kinds of wines are associated with Italy?

Red and white table wines, rosés, and dessert specialties. The red table wines are the most prolific. These can be light bodied or heavy bodied, astringently dry or semi-dry, mediocre or elegant.

525

Are Italian vineyards individually recognized?

Hardly. Italian tradition evolved along lines that bypassed or minimized the concept of individual properties. A classification system such as that of Bordeaux has never taken hold in Italy.

526

What is the format of Italian nomenclature?

Most Italian wines are identified by their geographic locale or origin. A few are named for grape varieties.

527

What is a secco *Italian wine?*

One that is dry.

528

What is an amabile *Italian wine?*

One that is semi-dry.

529

What is an abboccato *Italian wine?*

One that is unmistakably sweet.

530

What is a vecchio *Italian wine?*

Vecchio is Italian for "old" or "aged." An Italian wine that has been kept in cooperage for an extended period is referred to as a *vecchio.*

531

What is a frizzante *Italian wine?*

One that has a natural tingle brought about through malolactic fermentation. *Frizzante* is the Italian counterpart of the German *spritz* and the French *pétillance.*

532

What is a consorzio?

An Italian trade panel that prescribes and administers quality guidelines for a given district.

533

What is a contina sociale?

An Italian viticultural cooperative. Many small, independent growers and vintners have recently combined forces to form efficient, up-to-date joint ventures.

534

What is a denominazione di origine controllata?

An official Italian designation that guarantees authenticity of origin and adherence to a rigid production code. *Controllata* standards were enacted in 1967 and have done much to win greater esteem for fine Italian wines.

535

Does the phrase "Italia marchio nazionale" *have any special viticultural meaning?*

No. The words merely show that the merchandise is of Italian origin.

536

What is the significance of an I.N.E. neckband on a bottle of Italian wine?

The letters are loosely an abbreviation for "international export" and have no real viticultural meaning.

537

Which wine launched the Italian-wine boom in the United States?

Chianti, the fiasco (encased in straw) package that is seen wherever Italian cuisine is featured. From the late forties to the late sixties Chianti accounted for almost 10 percent of all the foreign wines sold in the United States. Although Chianti's share of the U.S. market has since declined, it is still one of the leading imported wines.

538

What is the true locale of Chianti wine?

Under present *controllata* decrees Chianti must come from Tuscany, in central Italy. Within this district Siena, Poggibonsi, Certaldo, Pistoia, Pontassieve, and Firenze (Florence) are viticultural centers.

539

What is a Colli Chianti?

Colli stands for "hill" or "slope." Tuscany is duly proud of six such vineyard zones: Rufina; Fiorentino (Florentine); Senesi (Siena); Aretini (Arezzo); Montal-bano (Mount Albano); Pisane (Pisan). Collectively these six zones make up what is officially known as the classical Chianti zone.

540

What is a Chianti Classico?

A Colli Chianti that has been barrel aged for two years. Maturity is essential to Chianti quality. A Chianti that has been bottled early may have a sharp, acrid edge. A *classico* has a velvety smoothness.

541

What is a Chianti riserva?

One that has been aged for three years before bottling. A *riserva* designation may also be used for other types of Italian wines.

542

What percentage of Chianti wines are of classico *or* riserva *status?*

Between 10 and 15 percent.

543

Are all Chianti wines fiasco packaged?

No. The Bordeaux-shaped fifth is coming into vogue for *classicos* and *riservas* in an effort to break away from the static Chianti stereotype. The skyrocketing cost of straw—from eight cents a unit to forty cents since 1973—has hastened the switch.

544

Is Chianti bottled in more sizes than other European wines?

Yes—half pint, three-quarter pint, pint, pint and a half, fifth, quart, half-gallon, gallon.

545

Does a design on a Chianti neckband have any special significance?

Most Chianti packages have some sort of colorful pictorial neckband. Only one design, however, has any official sanction—that of a black rooster on a gold and red background. Only a *Colli* Chianti from one of the six subdivisions of the classical zone may be so identified.

546

What is a camello *Chianti bottle?*

A fiasco bottle with an extremely tall neck. The neck may protrude from eighteen to fifty-four inches above the base of the container. These specially molded bottles are frequently displayed in Italian-American restaurants.

547

How many grape varieties are used in vinifying Chianti?

Usually four—three reds (Sangiovese, Canaiolo, and

Colorino) and one white (Trebbiano). The standard proportions are 70 percent Sangiovese and 10 percent each of the other three.

548
Is there such a thing as white Chianti?

This is a moot point. The controllata code grants official recognition only to red Chianti. The white companion wines are bottled as Toscana (Tuscany) Bianco.

549
What is the price of Chianti wines?

From $1.50 to $2.00 for a utility grade; double to triple that for a *colli*, *classico*, or *riserva*. These prices apply to the twenty-four-ounce or fifth size.

550
What is Aleatico?

A red dessert wine from Tuscany. The label may read, "Aleatico di Portoferraio," to avoid confusion between the Tuscany bottling and Aleatico di Puglia, which is from a district south of Tuscany. The Puglia product is also red but changes to orange with age.

551
What is Vinsanto?

A golden-amber dessert wine from Tuscany.

552
What is Italy's supreme grape variety?

Nebbiolo, a red grape that rivals France's Cabernet Sauvignon and Pinot Noir. Nebbiolo has flourished in the northwestern district of Piedmont for seven centuries.

553

Which Italian wine is the pinnacle of Nebbiolo vinification?

Barolo, a robust, full-bodied *vecchio*. The *controllata* code stipulates a minimum of three years' aging before bottling. Some Barolos are aged twice as long and even more. Barolo is one of the world's top-rated red table wines.

554

Which localities are Barolo centers?

The village of Barolo itself, plus the villages of Alba, La Morra, Castiglion, Faletto, Casteletto, Monforte, Perno, Grinzane, and Verduno.

555

What is Barbaresco?

Barolo's "kid brother," a half-step beneath Barolo in maturity and sophistication, but a superb wine in its own right.

556

Which localities are Barbaresco centers?

The villages of Barbaresco, Treiso, and Neive.

557

How does Nebbiolo wine differ from Barolo and Barbaresco?

A Nebbiolo varietal is a lighter-bodied bottling from the province of Cuneo. The *controllata* code dictates 100 percent Nebbiolo stock. The yield per acre, though, may be much greater than for Barolo and Barbaresco, and the fermented juice may be bottled after only one year in cooperage. At this age a Nebbiolo is a finished wine. By contrast, a Barolo or Barbaresco less than three years old would be noticeably deficient in body and character.

558

What is Spanna?

A Piedmont colloquialism for all Nebbiolo grapes except those set aside for Barolo and Barbaresco vinification.

559

What is Gattinara?

Piedmont village wine made from Spanna grapes or a combination of spanna and Croattina grapes.

560

What is Ghemme?

A Piedmont village wine made from Nebbiolo stock.

561

What is Barbera?

A red table wine from the Asti and Cuneo zones of Piedmont. Barbera vines may sprout two to three times as many clusters as Nebbiolo vines.

562

Why is the Barbera variety so named?

Barbera is Italian for "barber," or to stretch the idiomatic vernacular, "in need of a shave." The skin of this red grape has a fuzz akin to that of a peach.

563

Does Barbera respond to aging?

Yes. The grape is vinously powerful. A pronounced "bite" will come through if the fermented liquid is withdrawn from the barrel in less than two years.

564

What is Freisa?

An abundant Piedmont varietal wine. Freisa—a light young, fragrant beverage—is the Italian version of Beaujolais.

565

What is Grignolino?

A red grape species that grows in a narrowly confined area close to Asti. As a varietal bottling, Grignolino is a light-bodied, mellow beverage noticeably enhanced by eighteen to twenty-four months of maturation.

566

What is Dolcetto?

A pleasant red table wine from the Alba area of Piedmont. Dolcetto, Grignolino and Freisa are collectively spoken of as the soft, delicate red wines of Piedmont.

567

Are any other Piedmont red wines worthy of mention?..

Yes. Brachetto and Carema. These are small-scale bottlings that are occasionally exported to the United States. Brachetto is suggestive of a semi-dry Rosé. Carema is a heavier, darker wine.

568

Does Piedmont produce any distinguished white table wines?

Yes. Cortese, from the grape of that name, is an excellent white wine. Cortese is a light, mild, gentle wine.

569

Do prime Piedmont zones have common topography?

Yes. The choicest vines are planted on slopes, terraces, and hillside plots. Such sites afford the proper kind of drainage and exposure to sunlight.

570

What is Asti's primary claim to viticultural fame?

Sparkling wine, or Asti Spumante, is one of the world's most famous effervescent wines.

571

What is the grapestock of Asti Spumante?

Muscat is the predominant variety. Dashes of Cortese, Erbaluce, Riesling, and Prosecco may be incorporated for flavor and aroma balance.

572

How does Asti Spumante differ from French champagne?

Asti Spumante is milder (7 to 10 percent alcohol by volume), sweeter, livelier, and more aromatic.

573

Is Asti Spumante's sweetness the result of dosage?

No. Its delightful sweetness is entirely natural. The Muscat grape imparts this quality.

574

Does Asti Spumante require extensive bottle aging?

No. The beverage is ready for consumption soon after the completion of secondary fermentation. At this stage the wine is fully developed. Aging would, in fact, detract from its fresh, lively, fragrant dimensions.

575

Is Asti Spumante less expensive than French Champagne?

Considerably. Top-grade bottlings are available at about six dollars. Two factors are responsible for this comparative economy—the predominant vinestock is a prolific bloomer, and the much shorter aging period cuts storage and handling costs.

576

Of what value is a vintage year with regard to Asti Spumante?

Absolutely none.

577

Is Asti the only authenticated Spumante zone?

No. Alessandria and Cuneo are also official zones of origin.

578

Is Piedmont associated with any other sparkling wines?

Yes. Nebbiolo Spumante, a red, mild, effervescent wine that is a bit drier than Asti Spumante.

579

What is the viticultural importance of the Turin zone of Piedmont?

Turin is, and has been since 1786, the supreme zone for Italian Vermouth.

580

What is Vermentino?

A dry white varietal wine. Its origin is Liguaria (the Italian Riviera), which lies between Tuscany and Piedmont on the Mediterranean. Genoa and San Remo are in Liguria.

581

What is Cinqueterre?

Literally, "five lands." To the south of Genoa are five mountainous communes collectively grouped as Cinqueterre. The wine so named is an attractive white wine. There are two versions—a dry and a semi-dry.

582

Where is Lombardy?

To the east of Piedmont, near the Swiss border. Milan is in Lombardy.

583

Is the topography of Lombardy more comparable to that of Piedmont or Liguria?

No area of Italy can quite duplicate Piedmont's gently rolling terrain. Lombardy and Liguria sites are essentially craggy, rocky inclines.

584

What is Lombardy's most prestigious wine?

Valtellina, a robust dry red from the valley of the same name. The wine stock is Chiavennasca, a Nebbiolo off-shoot.

585

Which Valtellina localities are considered superior?

Grumello, Inferno, Sassella, and Valgella.

586

Do any other grapes of Piedmont ancestry grow in Lombardy?

Yes. Barbera, Cortese, and Croattina. These species fare well in Lombardy, although somewhat less admirably than in their native Piedmont habitat.

587

Which red-grape varieties are indigenous to Lombardy?

Ughetta and Uva Rara, both of which mix exceedingly well with Croattina and barbera.

588

What is Val Versa?

A dry white wine from the Versa Valley town of Pavia in Lombardy. Val Versa is vinified from a combination of Riesling and Cortese grapes.

589

What is Lugana?

A light-bodied dry white wine from the Lake Garda sector of Lombardy.

590

Which Lombardy subdivision is identified with rosé wines?

The western embankment of Lake Garda. Lake Garda rosés are dry, light bodied, and fragrant. They are meant to be consumed young.

591

How are Lake Garda rosés labeled?

As Chiaretto or Chiarello, with or without such appendages as Rosé, Rosato, or del Garda.

592

Is the eastern shore of Lake Garda viticulturally fertile?

Marvelously so. Here lies the Verona district, famous for excellent dry reds and dry whites.

593

Which Veronese village wines are noteworthy?

Bardolino, Valpolicella, and Soave. The first two are dry reds; the last is a dry white. These wines are decidedly softer than those of Piedmont.

594

Is there an affinity between Valpolicella and Valpantena?

Yes. They are adjoining valley settlements north of Verona. The wines of either village are fundamentally alike—so much so, in fact, that Valpantena has been accorded the right to assume a Valpolicella *denominazione di origine.*

595

What is Recioto?

A red Veronese wine vinified from grapes hand picked from the top or the outside of the cluster. This layer has absorbed extra sunlight. Such over-ripe grapes are ideally suited for *vecchio* vatting and yield a wine with a velvety depth.

596

What is the distinction between Recioto Amabile and Recioto Amarone?

Amabile is a sparkling red wine processed from sun-drenched grapes with a higher level of natural sweetness. Amarone is a still wine whose vine stock has fermented into a drier beverage.

597

What is Gambellara?

A Veronese white wine that bears a family resemblance to Soave.

598

Where is the Tyrolean zone of Italy?

In the northeastern corner of the country. The zone is subdivided into Trentino-Alto Adige and Friuli-Venezia Giulia.

599

Does the viticultural background of the Tyrolean zone differ from that of the rest of Italy?

Yes. The Tyrol is German oriented, owing to its early status as a pawn in military battle. There is also a

French undercurrent, a vestige of the Napoleonic era. The prevailing grape varieties are descended from both countries.

600

Which varietal wines are vinified in the Tyrol?

Among the dry reds are Cabernet and Merlot. The dry whites include Traminer, Pinot Bianco, and Riesling.

601

What is Verduzzo?

An excellent white table wine from Friuli-Venezia Giulia.

602

What is Tyrolean Tocai?

A white table wine that differs from other Tyrolean bottlings in that it has a noticeably tangy nuance.

603

What is Teroldego?

A choice Tyrolean dry red wine.

604

What is Terlano?

A superior dry white wine from the Tyrolean town of Terlaner.

605

What is Santa Maddalena?

A superb red table wine produced in Trentino-Alto Adige.

606

What is the price range of the wines of northern Italy?

Generally from two dollars and change to four dollars and change. Vecchio wines vinified from Nebbiolo grapes may run as high as nine dollars.

607

Which provinces besides Tuscany are situated in central Italy?

Emilia Romagna, Marche, Lazio, and Umbria.

608

What is Emilia Romagna's claim to viticultural fame?

Lambrusco, a fragrant, charming, semi-dry frizzante red wine. The wine is named for a grape species that flourishes near the city of Bologna. Lambrusco's depth of flavor and delightful tingle have engendered mass appeal in the United States.

609

What is Sangiovese?

A dry red Emilia Romagna varietal. The Sangiovese grape imparts a rustic hardiness.

610

What is Albana?

The white counterpart of Sangiovese. Albana is an uncomplicated, down-to-earth "peasant" wine.

611

Which wine is synonymous with Marche?

Verdicchio, a lively, light-bodied white varietal. A

verdicchio made from the cream of the harvest may be bottled as a verdicchio dei Castelli di Jesi.

612

Which wine put Lazio on the enological map?

Est! Est! Est! a dry white wine made in the town of Montefiascone, near Rome. The exclamatory name is said to stem from a German bishop's trek to the Vatican. A member of the clergyman's retinue was dispatched as an advance agent to scout inns along the route that purveyed victuals and libation fit for the bishop's party. An "Est" (It is) placard was to be placed at the entrance of those which passed the test. One Montefiascone inn was found to be so extraordinary that three placards instead of one were set on its grounds.

613

What is Orvieto?

An Umbrian white wine that can be vinified as a crisply dry or semi-dry beverage. The vineyards that encircle the ancient city of Orvieto harvest the finest white grapes in all of central Italy.

614

Are the central Italian provinces of Abruzzo and Molise enologically significant?

No. The vineyards of these Adriatic provinces cultivate table grapes, rather than wine grapes.

615

What is the Latium zone?

A network of volcanic hills a few miles south of Rome.

This zone is sometimes referred to as Castelli Romani, or the Roman Hills.

616

What kind of wines are Latium, or Castelli Romani, wines?

Simple, prosaic, everyday whites and reds. Latium bottlings are the "house" wines featured in many of Rome's family restaurants.

617

Are Latium localities individually identified?

Yes. The most famous of the Castelli Romani centers is Frascati. Frascati wines are in wide distribution in the United States. The villages of Genzano, Grottaferrata, Lanuvo, Marino, and Velletri are also worthy of mention.

618

Does Latium produce any varietals?

Yes, Cesanese. This is a pleasant, utilitarian red table wine.

619

What is Trebbiano?

A white varietal wine from central Italy. Trebbiano vines bloom especially well in Emilia Romagna and Lazio.

620

How expensive are the wines of Emilia Romagna, Marche, Lazio, and Umbria?

From $1.50 to $3.50.

621

Which provinces comprise the southern tier of the Italian mainland?

Puglia, on the Adriatic; Campania, on the Mediterranean; and Calabria, on both coasts by virtue of its geographic setting as the narrowest part of the Italian boot.

622

How productice is Puglia?

Acre for acre, Puglia is probably the most productive province in Italy.

623

What are the leading wine villages of Puglia?

Alberobello, Brindisi, Cerignola, Salento, and Taranto, in the districts of Apulia and Lucania.

624

Are Puglia wines well-known in the United States?

Despite their tremendous abundance, the wines of Puglia have had only minor impact here. Until just a few years ago the vintners of Apulia and Luciana were bulk-oriented. Millions of gallons were shipped to northern suppliers for blending and processing. A trend toward greater involvement with the finished package is beginning to take hold in Puglia. Unprecedented emphasis is being placed upon methodology and technology. Puglia bottlings of refinement and finesse can be expected to make their presence felt as time goes on.

625

Which Puglia table wines have the innate capacity to be successfully promoted in the United States?

Castel del Monte (red, white, rosé), Locorotondo (white), Martina Franca (white), Ostuni (white), Sansavero (white), Santo Stefano (red), Torre-Quarto and Giulia (red and white).

626

Are any dessert wines vinified in Puglia?

Yes. The Aleatico cited earlier in connection with the Aleatico of Piedmont, plus an array of Moscato (Muscat) formulations. The dessert wines of Puglia are aromatic, flavorful, and smooth. Blended with botanicals, the end product can be a vinous ambrosia.

627

Is Calabria viticulturally important in the American marketplace?

Not at the moment. It would not be far-fetched, however, to prognosticate that three splendid red table wines—Pellaro, Pollino, and Savuto—will attract admirers here before long.

628

Is Campania familiar to many Americans?

Yes. The Bay of Naples, Mount Vesuvius, the Amalfi coastline, and dozens of scenic waterways and villages are tourist meccas.

629

What is Campania's most celebrated wine?

Lacrima Christi (tears of Christ). This is an exquisite dry white wine available in either still or sparkling form.

630

Are any other white table wines vinified in Campania?

Yes—Avellino and Fiano.

631

What are Campania's most notable red table wines?

Gragnano, Solopaca, and Taurasi. All three improve appreciably after several years in the barrel. Taurasi, in particular, takes on classic dimension with five to six years of vatting.

632

What is Ravello?

A Campanian village wine that may be vinified as a dry white, dry red, or rosé.

633

Do the Naples Bay islands produce any wine?

Yes. Two lovely dry white wines are named for the off-shore settlements of Capri and Ischia.

634

Has the island of Sardinia made contributions to Italian enology?

Yes. Sardinian vintners have mastered the art of formulating dessert specialties. Nasco (white), Giro, and Monica (both red) are tributes to this expertise. These are smooth, velvety, sweet elixirs with an intriguing aroma and a beguiling aftertaste.

635

What is Vernaccia?

An amber-tinted dessert specialty that exemplifies the height of Sardinian enological skill. Vernaccia is vinified from sun-drenched grapes that undergo slow, prolonged fermentation. The finished product has a wispy lightness and a captivating natural sweetness.

636

Does Sardinia bottle any table wines?

Yes, two rather good ones—Nuragus (white) and Oliena (red).

637

Is the Island of Sicily a vineyard haven?

Definitely. Wine is a major commodity on this sunny island. The Sicilian harvest is diversified, rich and abundant.

638

What are the outstanding wine localities in Sicily?

Agrigento, Catania, Lipari, Messina, Mount Etna, Palermo, Pantelleria, Syracuse, and Trapani.

639

Which grape varieties thrive in Sicily?

Cateratto Lucido, Greciano, Grillo, Inzolia, Muscat (Moscato), Nerello Muscalese, and Zibibbo.

640

What is Sicily's most renowned wine?

Marsala, a fortified wine with a base suggestive of Sherry.

641

Is Marsala production confined to certain sectors of Sicily?

Yes. The western zones of Palermo, Trapani, and Agrigento are officially sanctioned. Western Sicily has through the years become arbitrarily known as Marsala. This geographic notation may appear on a label with or without reference to Palermo, Trapani, or Agrigento.

642

Is it permissible to add flavoring agents to marsala?

Yes. Infusing the base liquid with such natural additives as eggs, almonds, or strawberries is an ancient Sicilian tradition.

643

What is mamertino?

A dessert specialty from eastern Sicily. Mamertino is golden yellow and intensely aromatic.

644

Which Sicilian table wines are of better-than-average quality?

Etna (red and white), from the mountainous terrain and lava-enriched soil of Mount Etna; eloro (red and white), from Syracuse; faro (red), from Messina. All three zones are in eastern Sicily.

645

What is Segesta?

A dry red village wine from western Sicily. Segesta is a robust, assertive wine.

646

How do the wines of southern Italy compare in price with those of central Italy?

They are in the same general range. The majority of the wines in both regions are priced at less than $3.50.

647

Which country stands next to Italy and France in annual gallonage?

Spain. More than 10 percent of the world's total wine gallonage is bottled in Spain.

648

What is Spain's most famous dessert wine?

Sherry, which is native to the delimited district of Jerez in southern Spain. No other Spanish or European district may process or market Sherry.

649

Which varieties are known as Sherry grapes?

Palomino and Pedro Ximinez. These species fare exceedingly well in the chalky, powdery soil of Jerez.

650

Is Sherry a blended wine?

Very much so. The character of the finished product is the outcome of a marriage of a number of separate vattings. Palomino and Pedro Ximinez are unpredictable grapes. It is impossible to foretell precisely how a given pressing will turn out. Blending is therefore necessary for balance, uniformity, and consistency.

651

What is the solera system of Sherry blending?

A technique of blending older and younger wines of the same overall characteristics. From four to eight casks are grouped together in sequence according to age with the least mature and the most mature wines at either end. Cask number one (the youngest wine) is half-emptied and replenished with liquid held in cask number two. The liquid required to fill cask number two is drawn from cask number three—and so on up the line. The last vessel winds up containing an even mixture of the oldest and youngest Sherries.

652

Can a solera system be maintained perpetually?

Yes. It is not at all startling to come across Spanish Sherries that embody a measure of wine from a solera started in the nineteenth century.

653

How many cases of wine can be packaged from a solera run-off?

Each cask, or butt, has a capacity of 100 to 125 gallons. Half of the contents is withdrawn per bottling. This works out to twenty to twenty-five cases per butt in the solera system. A winery specializing in this aging and blending process would therefore have to keep scores of solera systems in simultaneous operation.

654

At what intervals is the newest solera barrel replaced?

Usually every second or third year. The replacement barrel has been in reserve for several seasons so that even the youngest wine in a solera-blended Sherry could readily hold its own as a finished entity.

655

What are the two broad classifications for Spanish Sherry?

Fino and Oloroso. The former is lighter (a pale amber as opposed to a dark amber) and somewhat drier, although Sherry is a sweet wine.

656

Which Spanish Sherry bottlings are Finos?

Fino itself, plus amontillado and Manzanilla.

657

Which Spanish Sherry bottlings are Olorosos?

Oloroso itself, plus Amoroso and Cream.

658

What is Spanish Brown Sherry?

An Oloroso type which has gained wider acceptance in England than in the United States.

659

What is a Spanish Flor Sherry?

Flor is a yeast coating that forms on the top of some Sherries during fermentation and aging. A *Flor* liquid will yield a Fino, rather than an Oloroso.

660

Does the nutlike aftertaste of some Spanish Sherries come from the vinestock?

No. This dimension develops through natural or artificial heat. The liquid may be "baked" in bulk, or the barrel may be placed outdoors to bask in the sun. Temperatures topping one hundred degrees occur regularly in Jerez.

661

Must a Spanish Sherry be bottled in Spain?

No. The wine must be produced in Jerez from native vinestock. Packaging, however, may be done abroad. Some of the most familiar brands of Spanish Sherry are bottled in England.

662

How widely do Spanish Sherry prices vary?

A good bottling may be purchased for $2.50 to $3.50. A superb one may cost more than double that.

663

Is southern Spain the origin of any other dessert wines besides Sherry?

Yes. Muscatel, which is heavy-bodied and amber, is vinified in Jerez. Málaga, a locality near Jerez, is associated with an aromatic, reddish-brown dessert speciality. Jerez and Málaga are both in Andalusia.

664

What is Spain's most prominent table wine region?

Rioja, a northeastern region named for the Oja river (Río Oja). Rioja is separated from France by the Pyrenees Mountains.

665

Which Rioja inner districts are important wine centers?

Alavesa, Alfaro, Alta, Baja, Haro, and Logroño. Baja is more involved with crops than with vinification. Its name is seldom linked with a finished product.

666

How productive is the Rioja region?

Very. Output averages twenty million cases annually.

667

Which grape varieties are indigenous to Rioja?

Calagraño, Garnacha, Graciano, Mazuelo, Monastrel, Tempranillo, and Viura.

668

Does Rioja rank individual properties?

No. The evaluation of specific tracts, as in Bordeaux, would be rather meaningless. No individual vineyard is singularly distinguished (or undistinguished) compared with other parcels.

669

Is Rioja a blended wine?

Very much so. A liberal mix of juices is required for the ideal interplay of sugar, acid, color, and bouquet.

670

Is estate bottling widespread in Rioja?

No. The division between agriculture and vinification goes a long way back. As a rule the grower bows out of the picture after the pressing of the harvest. The yields of dozens of farmers or of a whole settlement may be contracted to a single supplier. Fermentation, aging, blending, packaging, and marketing are carried out under his auspices.

671

Does Rioja observe geographic controls?

Yes. All Rioja wines are governed by a *garantía de origen* which dates back to the sixteenth century.

672

Is a garantía de origen *a quality guarantee?*

No, merely an official declaration that the wine is wholly of Rioja origin.

673

What is a Rioja R. E. Number?

The letters stand for *registrar embotellar*, or "registered bottling house." Rioja bottlers are government licensed, inspected, and regulated. The registry number of the bottle is shown on the label.

674

How long must a Rioja wine be aged before it is bottled?

A minimum of one year. After three or four years of vatting a Rioja red will emerge as a smooth, well-balanced wine of discernible finesse. A *Blanco* (white) or *Rosado* (rosé) will reach its peak of perfection in half that time.

675

Will a Rioja wine necessarily improve with extended vatting?

No. A Rioja that has been in cooperage for six or eight

years may tend to have a bit of a dull, "woody" taste. Some Riojas seen here suffer from too long a vatting period.

676

Will a Rioja wine respond to bottle aging?

Yes. Reds, especially, may be enhanced by a year or so of undisturbed storage after three or four years of vatting.

677

What is a cosecha?

A Rioja vintage designation. It should be stressed that the *cosecha* year may be of dubious importance because the Rioja harvest does not experience radical fluctuations from season to season.

678

What is a Rioja Reserva?

A bottling that a supplier considers to be of superior stature. Although the term does not imply any official status, it may at times offer a clue to some of Rioja's better wines.

679

Does any other border region of Spain produce good table wines?

Yes—Galicia, in the northwestern part of the country near the Portugese border. Two excellent wine districts are found here—Ribero and Valdeorras.

680

Does any interior region of Spain produce good table wines?

Yes. La Mancha, in central Spain below Madrid and

Toledo. Especially noteworthy are the wines from the localities of Manzanares and Valdepeñas.

681

Which coastal region of Spain is noted for an abundance of better-than-average table wines?

Catalonia, which extends along the Mediterranean coast near Barcelona. Some of Spain's oldest and largest wineries are based in Catalonia.

682

Which Catalonian localities have achieved viticultural recognition?

Priorato, Reus, Sitges, Tarragona, and Villafranca del Panadés.

683

Are any other eastern-Mediterranean localities of Spain worthy of mention?

Yes—Alella, Alicante, Perelada, and Valencia.

684

Which native grape varieties bloom beyond Rioja?

Albillo, Bobal, Caino, Cencibel, Corifiena, Godelho, Macabeo, Monastrel, Muncia, Nova, and Planta.

685

Are any Spanish table wines made from classic French grape varieties?

Yes. One Spanish winery specializes in the cultivation and vinification of Cabernet Sauvignon, Pinot Noir, and Pinot Chardonnay. These offerings are available in the United States for less than five dollars a bottle.

686

May a Spanish table wine be generically labeled?

No. Some non-Rioja bottlings exported to the United States used to be labeled as Burgundy, Sauterne, or Chablis. In April 1973, the United States Treasury Department declared this practice to be misleading. For some strange reason the ruling applies only to wines from Spain.

687

What is a bodega?

Literally, a Spanish wine cellar. In colloquial usage a *bodega* may denote a wine merchant, producer, broker, agent, bottler, or shipper. Curiously, the word in the Latin American dialect heard in the United States means a grocery store.

688

What is a bota?

A traditional Spanish wine bag or wine pouch. It is made of the skin of an animal and is topped by a narrow pouring insert. The bota is held a few inches from the mouth and the liquid is squirted into the mouth by pressing the bag.

689

What is Sangría?

A prepared mixture of Spanish red table wine and citrus juices. This delightful concoction was introduced to the American public at the New York World's Fair in 1964–65 and has since become tremendously popular in this country.

690

Is Sangría's popularity predicated on its flavor alone?

No. Sangría's (also spelled "Sant'gría") mildness (as low as 7 percent alcohol by volume), economy (less than two dollars a bottle), and its presentation as a "party" or "fun" beverage have also been plus factors.

691

Are Spanish table wines economical?

Yes. Many fine bottlings can be had for $2.00 to $2.50. The very best offerings seldom exceed $4.50. Spanish viticulture has remained free of status-symbol forces that tend to have an inflationary effect.

692

What is a mesa wine?

Any and all Spanish and Portuguese table wines may be so termed. *Mesa* is "table" in both languages.

693

Which wine is to Portugal as Sherry is to Spain?

Port, a red dessert wine from the controlled and delimited Douro River area in northeastern Portugal. As with Sherry, the actual bottling may take place in England.

694

Which Douro municipalities are closely affiliated with Port?

Oporto (from which comes the name) and Vila Nova da Gaia. These are on opposite banks of the Douro.

695

What is the vinestock of Port?

Bastardo, Mourisco, Tinta Cão, Tinta Francisca, and Touriga.

696

How does the soil of the Douro area differ from that of the rest of Portugal?

Douro soil contains soft rocks that crumble and become almost powdery. This soil composition provides the kind of drainage vital to the growth of the aforementioned varieties. The soil of other Portuguese areas is granite-laden.

697

What is a vintage Portuguese Port?

The adjective, of course, implies that the vinestock is wholly of a given year. They way in which a vintage port ages is of special interest. The liquid is bottled after only two or three years of vatting. The wine, however, will continue to improve in the bottle for at least another three years. In some cases the wine will remain in glass in the cellar for twice as long before being shipped.

698

What is Crusted Port?

A bottle-aged Port that throws off a hardened sediment. Tedious straining notwithstanding, some grape particles (lees) do escape the human eye when the wine is transferred from wood to glass for further maturation. As the years pass a solidified cake or crust may attach itself to the side of the bottle. There are Port enthusiasts who seek out this crust as a sign of proper bottle aging.

699

Is there such a thing as white Portuguese Port?

Yes. A nominal quantity of Douro fortified wine is processed from white grapes of the Rabigato and Verdelho species.

700

What is Madeira?

A Portuguese island off the North African coast. Madeira wine bears a resemblance to Sherry, rather than Port.

701

Is Madeira processed in a unique manner?

Yes. After fermentation the wine is stored for several months in a steamroom (*estufa*) where the temperature is maintained at approximately one hundred degrees. This treatment imparts an overtone suggestive of Sherry and enables the finished product to stand up admirably well for decades.

702

How are Madeira bottlings categorized?

From the palest to the richest as follows: Sercial; Boal (Bual), Verdelho, Malmsey. The first three are dessert varietals. Malmsey is made from Malvasia grapes.

703

What is Rainwater Madeira?

A general term of reference for a blended pale Madeira. The implication is that the wine is as soft as rainwater.

704

What is Portugal's best mesa region?

Dão (prnounced "Dawn") in central Portugal. Dãos are extremely pleasant, smooth, well-balanced wines that attain their peak of perfection with three years of vatting. Perhaps 95 percent of the wine from this region is red.

705

Which Dão municipalities are viticultural centers?

Coimbra, Guarda, and Viseu. These three municipalities form a triangle around the region.

706

Which grape varieties flourish in Dão?

Arinto Tourigo, Dona Branca, Preto Mortágua, Tinta Pinheira, and Tourigo.

707

How do Dão wines differ from Rioja wines?

As a class they are generally somewhat more full-bodied, more robust, and richer.

708

What is Pinhel?

A village between the Dão region and the Douro river region. Pinhel table wines are just a cut below Dão bottlings.

709

What is Colares?

A "freak" vineyard belt a few miles northwest of Lisbon. Much of the vineyard property lies in sand dunes.

Grapes will not propagate in this kind of sub-soil. The roots of the vinestock must therefore be set in trenches six to eight feet below the ground.

710

Is Colares a blended wine?

No. Only one grape variety is planted in the trenches of Colares—the red Ramisco.

711

Is the Ramasco variety a vineyard "freak"?

Yes. Its juice is one of the world's slowest to metamorphose into wine. At times a finished taste may not assert itself for four to five years. Moreover, the process of transformation is unpredictably erratic. One batch of wine may turn out unpalatable while another turns out beautifully.

712

What is Bucelas?

A utilitarian, semi-dry white wine from a village near Colares.

713

What is Setúbal?

A viticultural settlement on the Atlantic coast a short distance from Lisbon. Setúbal lends its name to a sweet white wine a little less intense than most dessert wines?

714

What is Carcavelos?

A town near Setúbal associated with an agreeable red dessert wine.

715

What is Torres Vedras?

The viticultural center of a large coastal region north of Lisbon—Estremadura. This region produces a plentiful supply of everyday, utilitarian red and white table wines.

716

What is Vinho Verde?

A *mesa w*ine from the northwest corner of Portugal. *Verde* is Portuguese for "green." The adjective in this context refers not to a wine that is not sufficiently mature or ready for bottling, but to a young wine (usually white) that is light, mild, fresh, and lively.

717

What sets Vinho Verde *apart from other Portuguese* mesa *wines?*

Its malolactic *pétillance,* or tingle. *Vinho Verde* needs only several months of vatting. At this stage malolactic fermentation invests the liquid with a refreshing crackle, which is sustained when the wine is transferred from wood to glass.

718

Which type of wine has revolutionized Portugal's viticultural standing in the United States?

Rosé. Since the mid-sixties overall importation of wine has tripled. The importation of Portuguese Rosés, however, has increased more than tenfold.

719

To what can the ascent of Portuguese Rosés be attributed?

To an urgently felt consumer need for a versatile, uncomplicated, reasonably priced wine with mass taste appeal. Portuguese Rosés provided the perfect answer at a perfectly timed period of consumer searching. Here was the ideally correct choice for any type of cuisine or social setting.

720

Is Rosé production confined to any one area of Portugal?

No. Although Azeitao, Lisbon, Oporto, and Sangalhos have emerged as trade centers, geography is not a monumental issue. Suitable vinestock is ubiquitous. The expertise that attends crushing, *cuvaison*, fermentation, and blending plays a more decisive role.

721

Do Portuguese Rosé bottlings resemble one another?

Up to a point. Beyond a group likeness, though, there are perceptible variations. No Portuguese Rosé is really robust, but some are a trifle heavier-bodied than others. No Portuguese Rosé is really sweet, but some are a trifle sweeter (or less dry) than others. Such differences are matters of personal taste preferences and not yardsticks of quality.

722

How much do Portuguese wines cost?

A good Port can run as much as a good Sherry. Table wines, including rosés, are in the two- to four-dollar bracket.

723

What is a quinta?

A Portuguese vineyard.

724

What is consumo?

A Portuguese term for native wines consumed mostly by peasants, farmers, and rural artisans.

725

What is a colheita?

A Portuguese vintage designation.

726

What is a Garrafeira *Portuguese wine?*

One that the supplier set aside for further bottle maturation because of the extraordinary taste elements it showed during vinification.

727

What is trabalhador?

The almost extinct Portuguese (and Spanish) practice of pressing grapes by stomping on them with the bare feet.

728

Has Portugal made a non-vinous contribution to the world of wine?

Yes. Portugal is the source of practically all of the corks used worldwide in packaging.

729

What is a Monimpex wine?

A Hungarian wine. Monimpex is Hungary's central viticultural cooperative.

730

Which grape varieties grow in Hungary?

Furmint, Keknyelu, and Pinot Gris (white); Kadarka and Voros (red).

731

What is Hungary's most acclaimed wine?

Tokay, an amber dessert wine. The town of Tokay (Tokaj) is in northern Hungary at the approach to the Carpathian Mountains. The vinestock is Furmint.

732

What are Aszu grapes?

The Hungarian counterpart of German *Beeren* grapes. These are sun-scorched Furmint bunches which have built up an accentuated level of natural sugar.

733

What is a puttono (puttony)?

A hand basket in which *aszu* grapes are collected. A favorable harvest may yield a dozen or so *puttonos* per acre. The juice of several "putts" (usually three, four, or five, as noted on the label) may be added to a barrel of regular Furmint extract. A numbered "putt" Tokay has an extra dimension of natural richness.

734

What is Tokay Szamoodni (Szamorodni)?

Szamoodni has to do with the idea of the whole crop as a single entity. There is no breakdown of proportions of plain Furmint, *Edes* (sweeter Furmint), or *Aszu* bunches. The presence of *Edes* and *Aszu* grapes makes Tokay Szamoodni a more luscious bottling than Tokay Furmint, as well as a more expensive one. Tokay Furmint is packaged in a twenty-three-ounce size at $3.50. Szamoodni and Puttonos Tokays are sixteen-ounce bottlings and run from $3.00 to $6.00.

735

What is Egri Bikavér?

A full-bodied red Hungarian table wine. *Egri* tells the locale—the town of Eger. *Bikavér* is a graphic epithet— "like the blood of a bull." The vinestock is Kadarka, from which Nemes Kadar wine is also vinified.

736

What is Szekszárdi Voros?

A red Hungarian table wine. The village and the grape species are tied together.

737

What is a Badacsonyi Hungarian wine?

One of two white table wines from Mount Badacsony, on Lake Balaton in southwestern Hungary. Badacsonyi Szürkebarát is a Pinot Gris bottling. *Szürkebarát* is an epithet for "Grey Friar," and the wine may be alternatively labeled as such. Badacsonyi Kéknyelü is a varietal wine.

738

What is Debroi Harslevelu?

A semi-dry white wine from the Hungarian municipality of Debro.

739

How much do Hungarian table wines cost?

Voros is a two-dollar wine. The others are three-dollar wines.

740

What sort of wines does Hungary's neighbor Yugoslavia export?

Serviceable, moderately priced red and white table wines.

741

Which grape varieties are under cultivation in Yugoslavia?

Adaptations of Gamay, Cabernet, Merlot, Pinot Noir, Pinot Blanc, Riesling (Rizling), Sylvaner, and Traminer, plus two indigenous growths, Sipon (white) and Prokupac (red).

742

What nomenclature pattern do Yugoslavian wines follow?

Geography and grape variety are linked together in a prepositional compound. A few typical examples: Gamay from Venac; Cabernet from Istria; Merlot from Slavonia; Pinot Noir from Ljubljana; Pinot Blanc from Zagreb; Riesling (Rizling) from Lutomer; Sylvaner from Maribor; Traminer from Radogna; Sipon from Ormoz; and Prokupac from Vranje.

743

Does Yugoslavia export any fermentable fruit crops?

Yes. Dalmatian cherries are utilized in top-grade American cherry-flavored wines. Dalmatia extends along the shores of the Adriatic Sea in southern Yugoslavia.

744

Do grapes grow in Turkey?

Yes, in tremendous abundance. Only three countries in the world produce more grapes than Turkey.

745

Is Turkey much of a wine-producing country?

No. Only 3 percent of Turkey's grape harvest is fermented. Turkey was a Moslem nation until a little more than a generation ago, and its taboo on alcoholic beverages remains strong.

746

Does the United States import any wines from Turkey?

Yes. Sungurlu, a semi-dry white wine, and Papaskarasi (Papazkarasi), a semidry red wine. Both are named for indigenous grape varieties.

747

Are any Bulgarian wines available in the United States?

Yes. Vinimpex, the state export agency, ships three fairly good table wines here: Cabernet (red) and Tamianka and Rikat (both white). These are priced at $2.00. The whites may also be shipped as *Spätlese* bottlings at $2.50.

748

What is Retsina?

A white Greek vinous specialty. Retsina is sweet, yet it is not fortified. The sweetness is caused by resin flavoring. This enological twist is said to have had its beginning in ancient Greece, where fermented grape juice was stored in resin-treated goatskin pouches.

749

What is Kokineli (Kokinelli)?

A resin-flavored Greek Rosé wine. Kokineli's sweetness is not quite as accentuated as that of Retsina.

750

What is Roditis (Roditys)?

A semi-dry Greek wine that can be vinified as a red or a rosé.

751

What is Robola?

A white Greek table wine.

752

What is Hymettus?

A light-bodied Greek table wine named for Mount Hymettus, near Athens. The white is seen more frequently than the red.

753

What is Pendeli?

A red Greek table wine that takes its name from a mountainous area near Athens.

754

What is Mantinia (Mantineia)?

A white table wine produced in the peninsular region of Greece.

755

What is Samos?

A sweet white wine from the Greek island of Samos. Samos is made from Muscat grapes.

756

What is Mavrodaphne?

A red Greek dessert wine. Mavrodaphne is a rich, premium grape variety that abounds in the peninsular region of Greece referred to as the Peloponnesus. Mavrodaphne wine is more expensive than other Greek bottlings —$4.00, compared with $2.50 to $3.50.

757

What is Commandaria (Commandarie) Saint John?

A Cypriot (island of Cyprus) dessert wine processed from sun-drenched Mavron and Xynisteri grapes. It is acknowledged to have the longest continuous production record (almost eight centuries) of any proper-name wine in the world. The Knights of the Order of Saint John, an English Templar militia during the Crusades, marched through Cyprus in the twelfth century. They were so captivated by one of the native wines that they "christened" it Commandaria Saint John in their honor. The wine is customarily aged in cooperage or massive stone crocks for six or eight years. Commandaria Saint John is in distribution in the United States for $4.25 a bottle.

758

Does Poland send any wines here?

Yes. Two flavored wines—Mead and Wishnik. Mead has a honey base and can be processed as an amber or as a red beverage. Wishnik is a cherry concoction. Mead and Wishnik are often laced with herbs, spices, and botanicals.

759

Is the Soviet Union viticulturally productive?

Yes. The Soviet Union's annual volume far surpasses that of the United States. The product mix takes in red and white table wines, dessert wines, and sparkling wines.

760

Which areas of the U.S.S.R. are the most verdant?

The Crimea, the Ukraine, Armenia, Azerbaijan, and Georgia. These are in the southern part of the country.

761

What are some of the grape varieties indigenous to the U.S.S.R.?

Bordo, Livadia, and Seperavi (red); Manadis, Mzvane, and Rka-Zitelli (white).

762

Do any classic European grape varieties bloom in the Soviet Union?

Yes—Cabernet Sauvignon, Pinot Noir, Riesling, Semillon, and Traminer.

763

Which dessert wine is considered the Soviets' best offering?

Massandra, a Crimean wine suggestive of a Sherry.

764

What are the outstanding sparkling wines of the U.S.S.R.?

Abrau-Durso, named for Lake Abrau and the River Don, near the Black Sea; Donski, named for the River Don; Kaffia, from the Crimea.

765

Does the Soviet Union export wines?

Yes. International trade statistics show that one-fourth of Soviet output is sent abroad. At this writing an Abrau-Durso sparkling wine marketed under a proprietary name is available in the United States. Unlike other European countries the Soviet Union does not abide by delimitation decrees; the sparkling wines it exports are sometimes blatantly labeled as Champagne. Negotiations are now underway with regard to the shipment of Soviet still wines to the United States.

766

What sort of wines come from Czechoslovakia?

Prosaic white table wines and fruit-flavored formulations. The latter include cherry, blackberry, raspberry, and strawberry wines.

767

Which grape variety dominates Luxembourg's viticulture?

Riesling. The wines of Luxembourg are suggestive of German Moselles. Luxembourg's Alzette River is, in fact a tributary of the Moselle.

768

Which of Luxembourg's settlements are viticultural centers?

Ehnen, Grevenmacher, Remich, Wasserbilig, Wintringen, and Wormedlingen.

769

Which grape species bloom in Austria?

Grüner Veltliner, Riesling, Rotgipfler, and Sylvaner. These are all white grapes. Token acreage of Gamay and Pinot Noir offshoots (red) is also under cultivation.

770

How many Austrian villages are viticulturally important?

Seven—Grinzing and Nussberg, on the outskirts of Vienna; Gumpoldskirchen and Vöslau, south of Vienna; and Dürnstein, Krems, and Loiben, west of Vienna on the banks of the Danube. Gumpoldskirchen is the one most familiar to American consumers.

771

Are Austrian Spätlese and Auslese bottlings of the same standing as German wines so labeled?

Not quite. Austrian grapes seem to benefit far less from late picking than do German grapes. Signs of extra ripeness are barely evident in the finished product. The Austrians, moreover, take these terms less seriously than do the Germans. Virtually all Austrian wines carry a "lese" notation. In the past the word cabinet was also invoked rather generally. The realization that most Austrian wines are on a single plane has curbed this practice.

187

772

What is Switzerland's prime viticultural area?
The Suisse Romande, which consists of the cantons of Neuchâtel, Valais, and Vaud. These are in French-oriented southwestern Switzerland.

773

What are the most abundant grape species of the Suisse Romande?
Chasselas, Fendant, and Johannisberg (white); Gamay and Pinot Noir (red).

774

Do Neuchâtel, Valais and Vaud share a common physical setting?
Yes. Their vineyards are planted on waterfront plots. Lake Neuchâtel is in Neuchâtel. The Rhône River touches Valais. Lake Geneva is in Vaud.

775

What type of wine is Neuchâtel?
A charming, light-bodied dry white wine.

776

What is Cortaillod?
A red village wine from the canton of Neuchâtel.

777

What is Oeil de Perdrix?
A pink wine from Neuchâtel sometimes packaged as Neuchâtel Rosé.

778

What is Dole?

A red Valais table wine. Gamay is the principal vine stock.

779

What is Fendant de Sion?

A white Valais table wine. Fendant is the grape variety. Sion is a town in Valais.

780

Are any wines named for subdivisions of Vaud?

Yes—Aigle, Chablais, Dézaley, La Côte, Lavaux, Saint-Saphorin, and Yvorne.

781

How do Swiss and Austrian wines compare in prices?

Swiss wines, as a group, are in the three- to four-dollar bracket—roughly one dollar higher than Austrian wines.

782

What is Denmark's claim to vinous fame?

Cherry-flavored proprietary wines. These have been well received throughout the world. Each is compounded according to a private recipe. Danish blackberry and strawberry specialties are marketed as well, but these lag far behind cherry proprietaries.

783

Do any grapes grow in the other Scandinavian countries?

No. Grapes cannot survive the frigid winters of Finland, Sweden, and Norway.

784

Are any English wines marketed in the United States?

Several offbeat fruit novelties, including bilberry, currant, and gooseberry, have been introduced here.

785

Does Ireland supply the United States with any wines?

No. Irish loganberries, however, go into American loganberry-flavored wines.

786

Does Scotland ship any wines to the United States?

A ginger-flavored specialty and a malt-accented novelty made their entries here a few years ago.

787

Is North Africa viticulturally productive?

Algeria, Morocco, and Tunisia are exceedingly verdant. The viticulture of these nations is something of an anomaly. The majority of the inhabitants disavow alcoholic beverages because of their Moslem convictions. But as French colonies they shipped millions of gallons of bulk wine (mostly *vin ordinaire*) to the motherland. As independent countries they are still struggling for success in international wine trade.

788

Are any North African wines seen in the United States?

Yes. Ait Mogai, Moghrabi (both come in red, white, and rosé), and Okapi (rosé only). These are fairly pleasant semi-dry wines from Morocco. They are in the three-dollar price category.

789

Does South Africa have a viticultural heritage?

Yes. Hordes of Huguenots took up residence in South Africa after their expulsion from France in the late sixteenth century. They brought with them vine cuttings and enological experience. Today's South African wine industry is carried on by their descendants.

790

What kinds of wines come from South Africa?

Dessert wines of the sherry family and red and white table wines. These are all of rather good quality.

791

What are South Africa's key vineyard zones?

Constantia, Montagu, Paarl valley, Robertson, Stellenbosch, Tulbagh, and Worcester. These are near Capetown.

792

Which grape varieties are indigenous to South Africa?

Steendruif and Sultana (white); Pontac and Shiraz (red).

793

Have any European varieties been cultivated successfully in South Africa?

Yes—Gamay, Cabernet Sauvignon, and Riesling.

794

What is Angola?

A semi-sweet wine from West Africa whose principal ingredient is fermented palm sap.

795

What is Benin?

A Nigerian wine made from native fruits and sap drawn from palm trees.

796

What is Yawa?

A West African palm wine.

797

What is Cajuada?

A West African wine made from raisins, native fruits, and cashew nuts.

798

Does Ethiopia produce wine?

Yes, almost three million cases a year, mostly dry reds similar in style to some of the lesser Italian wines. At this writing no Ethiopian wines are exported to the United States.

799

What are Ethiopia's most active wine centers?

Dukam, Gooder, and Holeta.

800

What is Australia's most productive wine regions?

Most of Australia's vineyard acreage lies in the southern part of the country. There are two main districts—the Hunter River Valley, north of Sydney, and the Barossa Valley, eight hundred miles west of Sydney near Adelaide.

801

Do these districts have any outstanding subdivisions?

Yes—Coonawarra Great Western, Murrumbidgee Valley, Murray Valley, and Tahbilk.

802

What grape varieties flourish in Australia?

Some of the better varieties of Spain, Italy, France, and Germany—Palomino, Dolcetto, Cabernet Sauvignon, Grenache, and Riesling.

803

What kinds of wine does Australia produce?

Exceptionally good dessert wines, top-notch table wines, and superb sparkling wines.

804

How are Australian table wines labeled?

Generically or after protoypes. Among those frequently seen in the United States are Burgundy, Chablis, claret, Moselle, Riesling, rosé, and Sauterne.

805

Is Australia actively engaged in international wine commerce?

Very much so. Australian wines are shipped to fifty-five countries. The popularity of Australian wines has been climbing steadily during the past decade.

806

Who is the father of Israeli viticulture?

Baron Edmond de Rothschild. Under his aegis model vineyards and wine cellars were established at the turn of the century. French vines and French technology characterized the initial thrust.

807

Have Israeli natives added another dimension to the country's viticulture?

Yes. The original French influence has been preciously retained. But to this the Sabras (native-born Israelis) have added expertise in dessert vinification. The motivation stemmed from the traditional hallowed use of sacramental wines in Hebrew religious observances. The Hebrew Sabbath is ushered in by partaking of sweet wine. Certain blessings, holidays, and milestone events are also commemorated in this fashion.

808

What are Israel's principal wine districts?

Rishon-le-Zion and Zikron-Yakov. These are near Tel-Aviv and Haifa, respectively.

809

What are Israel's predominant grape varieties?

For red table wines, Cabernet Sauvignon, Carignane, and Malbec. For white table wines, Sémillon and Sauvignon Blanc. Grenache is used for rosé vinification and for blending. Adaptations of Concord and Palomino garpes go into dessert wines.

810

How did Concord grapes find their way to Israel?

In the early days of the settlement a phylloxera plague threatened the young vineyards. New York State vines, which are immune to phylloxera, were imported for grafting with native roots. Through experimentation it was found that growing conditions favored Concord propagation.

811

Who controls Israel's wine industry?

80 percent of the wine shipped abroad is bottled by a public-service cooperative. Most of the profits are turned over to the government.

812

What is Almog?

A heavy-bodied, sweet red Israeli wine.

813

What is Topaz?

An amber Israeli dessert wine.

814

What is Partom?

An Israeli dessert wine similar in style to Port.

815

What is Sharir?

An Israeli dessert wine on the order of Sherry.

816

What is Savion?

An Israeli dessert wine suggestive of Hungarian Tokay.

817

What is Hadar?

An Israeli specialty wine made from native fruits, chiefly figs and dates.

818

What is Adom Atic?

A dry red Israeli wine. Adom Atic is a smooth, well-balanced table wine.

819

Is Israeli Concord a reasonable facsimile of American Concord?

An affinity is undeniable. Israeli Concord, though, seems to be a bit less grapy, or foxy. Although both wines are rich and flavorful, Israeli Concord has a softer accent.

820

Are the Arab nations viticulturally productive?

Hardly. The ancient art of enology has been virtually lost there. Present-day Egyptians, Syrians, and Jordanians are not wine drinkers, and despite reasonably good growing conditions, they have been unable to produce more than negligible quantities of wine suitable for export.

821

Does Taiwan ship any wine to the United States?

Yes—Shao-Hsing, an amber dessert wine, and Lychee, a nut-flavored specialty.

822

What is Sake?

A fermented Japanese rice beverage. Sake may occasionally be classified as a beer instead of a wine to qualify for an excise-tax advantage.

823

Does Sake serving involve a ritual?

Yes. The beverage is heated to a lukewarm temperature and poured into miniature cups à la demitasse. Sake is meant for group or party consumption.

824

Has the sake idea caught on here?

Not to any great extent. Despite the "fun" atmosphere in which sake is served, its somewhat vapid character has failed to stimulate mass interest in the United States.

825

Have any other Japanese wines become popular in the United States?

Yes. Japanese plum, cherry, and apple-honey wines have made inroads here. These have a sensory allure lacking in Sake.

826

Is Canada a vinous nation?

Yes. There are now seventeen operating wineries in Canada. These are modern, efficient installations equipped to turn out very palatable wines. Canadian output runs the full gamut from dry table wines to semi-sweet wines, from dessert wines to sparkling wines.

827

Which Canadian provinces are viticultural centers?

There are eight wineries in Ontario and six in British Columbia. Nova Scotia, New Brunswick, and Albert each have one. As far as gallonage goes, Ontario is out in front by a six-to-one margin.

828

What is Ontario's most verdant area?

The Niagara Valley. This vineyard belt covers twenty-one thousand acres on the north shore of Lake Ontario and is the domicile of fifteen hundred independent growers.

829

Can the Niagara Valley be equated with any U.S. area?

Yes, the Finger Lakes district of New York State. The two areas have much in common—soil, weather, proximity to water.

830

Which grape varieties are indigenous to both areas?

Catawba, Delaware, and Niagara.

831

Does Canada export wine grapes to the United States?

Yes. Scores of growers sell a share of their harvest to New York State vintners. A case in point is Catawba. It is not unusual to see a New York State supplier whose Catawba wine does not bear a New York State legend because the bottling contains more than 25 percent juice of Canadian origin.

832

What is a Canadian dinner wine?

A semi-sweet red, white, or pink wine. Canadian dinner wines have a Catawba or labrusca foxiness.

833

What is Manor Saint David?

A white Canadian table wine decidedly drier than a Canadian dinner wine and not nearly as grapy.

834

Which country leads the South American viticultural parade?

Argentina. Only three countries in the world bottle more wine than Argentina—France, Italy, and Spain. Argentina satisfies almost 10 percent of mankind's vinous needs, so that these four countries combined account for roughly 70 percent of the world's supply of wine. The bulk of Argentina's wine is of the table variety.

835

Do European grapes bloom in Argentina?

Yes—Pedro Ximinez, Malbec, Sémillon, and Riesling. There are also some offshoots of Burgundy and Piedmont vines.

836

What is Argentina's foremost native variety?

Criolla, which presses into an agreeable dry white wine.

837

What are the chief wine districts of Argentina?

Mendoza and San Juan. Two-thirds of the national output is from Mendoza; one-fourth comes from San Juan. Both are Andes Mountain districts.

838

What is the difference between Mendoza and San Juan wines?

San Juan wines, especially the reds, tend to be heavier, richer, and more robust. The much hotter summers of San Juan make the difference.

839

What are some of Argentina's less productive districts?

Cordoba, in central Argentina; Río Negro, in southern Argentina; Litoral, near Buenos Aires; and Occidente, in the northwestern part of the country.

840

How are the wines of Argentina labeled?

Without pretense or embellishment. The label tells the color of the wine (*blanco* or *tinto*) and its origin (Mendoza, San Juan, etc.). Control regulations forbid the use or adaptation of fancy European nomenclature.

841

What sort of wines does Argentina ship to the United States?

Two kinds. First, two-dollar wines plainly labeled as "ordinary." The "ordinary" wines of Argentina, though, are often far better than the term suggests. Second, three-to four-dollar wines with an unmistakable note of distinction.

842

How does Chile's European vinestock inventory differ from that of Argentina?

Chile has a much broader array of European varieties —Sauvignon Blanc, Pinot Blanc, Semillon, Cabernet Franc, Merlot, Malbec, Cabernet Sauvignon, Petit Verdot, Pinot Noir, and Riesling.

843

What is Chile's leading native grape variety?

Pais, which figures heavily in the production of utility-grade red table wines.

844

What is Chile's best table wine zone?

The central zone, which encompasses the Maipo Valley, the Aconcagua Valley, and the areas surrounding the cities of Valparaiso and Santiago.

845

What is Chile's best dessert wine zone?

The northern zone, which includes the districts of Atacama and Coquimbo. Muscat is the predominant variety.

846

How are Chilean wines labeled?

Generically, as Burgundy, Chablis, or Rhine; varietally, as Cabernet Sauvignon, Pinot, Noir, Sauvignon Blanc, or Riesling.

847

Does the Chilean government impose any extraordinary quality controls?

Yes. Each vineyard operates under an output ceiling. The yield beyond the assigned maximum may not be utilized for vinification. Thus, excessively dense planting, to achieve quantity at the expense of quality, would be futile.

848

What is a courant Chilean wine?

One that is at least a year old. No wine younger than that may leave the country.

849

How are older Chilean table wines designated?

A "Special" is two years old. A "Reserve" is four years old. A *"Gran Vino"* is more than four years old.

850

What is the shape of the traditional Chilean wine bottle?

The bocksbeutel shape, which is unlike the Bordeaux, Burgundy, or Rhine bottle in that it is short, squat, and oval.

851

How much do Chilean table wines cost?

From $2.50 to $4.00.

852

What are Brazil's key wine zones?

Rio Grande do Sul, Santa Caterina, Minas Gervais, and the territories encircling the cities of São Paulo and Rio de Janeiro.

853

What is Brazil's most prolific grape variety?

Strange as it may sound, Isabella is Brazil's most extensively planted vine. This is strange because Isabella is a transplanted American growth. Experimentation through the years has demonstrated that certain labruscas can fare well in the vineyards of Brazil.

854

Which other labrusca vines bloom in Brazil?

Concord, Delaware, Dutchess, and Niagara.

855

Which vinifera varieties are under cultivation in Brazil?

Barbera, Merlot, Riesling, and Trebbiano.

856

What is Brazil's product mix?

Utility table wines, premium table wines, excellent dessert wines, and outstanding sparkling wines. Some of Brazil's better offerings have recently begun reaching our shores.

857

Do any other South American nations produce wine?

Yes, Uruguay and Peru. Neither country exports wine

to the United States. Americans who have visited Peru speak glowingly of Tacama, a rosé reminiscent of a Tavel.

858

What is Mexico's viticultural profile?

Mexico produces about 1,500,000 cases a year, almost all of which is ordinary wine for local consumption. A decade of experimentation, however, has shown that Zinfandel, Pinot Chardonnay, Cabernet Sauvignon and Pinot Noir can be cultivated and vinified. Nominal quantities of these varietal wines are in distribution in California, Arizona and Oregon.

859

What is the world's most diversified wine region?

California. Here we find a viticultural melting pot with an amazing array of vines and wines from the lowliest to the lordliest.

860

How many grape varieties are planted in California?

Two hundred would be a conservative figure. Every major vine grown in Europe has been successfully transplanted in California. To this inventory must be added scores of other native and international species of which the following two dozen are representative: Aramon, Beclan, Black Malvoisie (Cinsaut), Clairette Blanche, Burger, Durif (Duriff), Feher Szagos, Fernao Pires, Flora, Gros Manzenc, Kleinberger, Marsanne, Marzemino, Melon, Meunier, Pagadebito, Raboso Piave, Refosco, Saint Macaire, Souzao, Teraldico, Tannat, Touriga, Valdepeñas and Verdot (Petite Verdot).

861

Has the number of California varieties hit a saturation plateau?

No, and it probably never will. Scientific hybridization and vinestock "intermarriage" beget new issues continually. The College of Agriculture of the University of California (at Davis) is the world's most advanced viticultural-research station. The work carried out here and elsewhere throughout California overshadows vinestock experimentation anywhere on earth.

862

Who is the father of California viticulture?

Count Agoston Haraszthy, a Hungarian nobleman and vineyardist. He was one of the coterie of Europeans who were drawn to California by its lush agricultural possibilities. To these immigrants we are indebted for launching California's wine industry. From 1850 to 1860 Haraszthy, an indefatigable experimenter, issued a stream or articles and treatises based on his research. So impressed was Governor John G. Downey that in 1861 he dispatched Haraszthy to Europe to purchase vinestock for commercial expansion. Haraszthy brought back 100,000 cuttings, which were planted in isolation and in fusion with native vines. So successful were Haraszthy's endeavors that California's production reached four million gallons by 1875 and fifteen million by 1895—a truly staggering accomplishment for those days.

863

Is all of California verdant?

Just about. Perhaps the only barren spot is a small

strip along the Mexican border. Here excessive aridity and poor irrigation are negative factors.

864

What are Mission grapes?

A family of nondescript varieties that wound up in California through the travels of Mexican and Spanish missionaries. These are low-bred grapes commonly relegated to the vinification of coarse fortified wines.

865

What is Thompson Seedless?

A commonplace white grape officially classified for table use but sometimes used viticulturally in low-level blending.

866

What is Ugni Blanc?

A California adaptation of Italy's Trebbiano variety.

867

What is Emerald Riesling?

A California cross-planting of Johannisberg Riesling (also known as White Riesling in California) and the Muscadelle.

868

Is Grey Riesling a form of Johannisberg Riesling?

No. It is descended from the Chauce (Chauche) Gris of France.

869

What is Barberone?

A California table wine thought to have been inspired by the Barbera species. The original composition may have been a mixture of red juices including Barbera.

870

What is White Pinot?

A California synonym for Chenin Blanc. As Chenin Blanc or White Pinot (not to be confused with Pinot Chardonnay) the wine is a creditable duplication of the very pleasant offerings of France's Loire valley.

871

Is Red Pinot related to Pinot Noir?

No. The former is Pinot Saint George, a California species. The latter is a classic grape of Burgundy lineage.

872

What is Ruby Cabernet?

An "intermarriage" of classic Cabernet Sauvignon and prolific Carignane vinestocks. The resultant species is a high-quality, high-yield California cross-planting.

873

What is Colombard?

A white grape variety of modest French descent that is sometimes seen as a California varietal entity.

874

What is Green Hungarian?

A California species that lends itself to an enjoyable white table wine. Despite the ethnic reference, the origin of the name is not precisely known.

875

Is there an affinity between California Tokay and Hungarian Tokay?

None whatever. California Tokay is a pinkish dessert wine. The vinestock is Flame Tokay, which has none of Furmint's majestic grace.

876

What is Angelica?

A white fortified California wine.

877

What is Muscatel?

A sweet, scented amber wine made from a grape of the Muscat family.

878

Which California Muscat grapes vinify into a superior wine?

Alexandria, Canelli, Frontignon, Hamburg, and Saint Laurent. The end product has a rich, luscious, liqueur-like quality.

879

Are Muscat grapes an international variety?

Yes. Vines of the Muscat family bloom generously in Mediterranean and South American countries as well as in California. The better wines made from these varieties are semi-sweet to sweet dessert types with an aromatic, full-bodied depth.

880

Is there a likeness between California Chianti and Italian Chianti?

It depends largely upon the vintner's expertise. California Chianti can be either a reasonable facsimile of the Tuscany beverage or a mediocre red table wine.

881

Does California Rhine wine resemble the German prototype?

Up to a point. Generally speaking, the German regional bottlings are a trifle lighter and livelier.

882

Is there a kinship between California Marsala and Marsala from Sicily?

There is an undeniable family likeness. The Italian product, however, is sometimes a bit richer.

883

What is Vino Rosso?

A California red table wine whose acidity and astringency have been modified by skillful blending. Vino Rosso has a slight touch of sweetness.

884

Is a California Mountain wine a premium bottling?

Not as a rule. A bottling so identified is usually a middle-of-the-road table wine.

885

What are the three major wine regions of California?

1. The Northern Coastal region, above and below San Francisco. Some of the choicest wines (especially varietals), of the United States come from here.

2. The Central Valley region, which runs from Sacramento to a point below Bakersfield, a distance of more than 275 miles. This region accounts for more than 60 percent of the wines made in the United States.

2. The Southern Coastal region, which encompasses the territory between Los Angeles and San Diego. The emphasis here is on serviceable dessert wines and light-bodied table wines.

886

What are the principal areas within these California regions?

Northern Coastal region: Alameda, Contra Costa, Guerneville, Livermore, Mendocino, Monterey, the Napa Valley, Oakville, Rutherford, San Benito, Saint Helena, Santa Clara, Santa Cruz, Santa Rosa, Saratoga, Solano, San Luis Obispo, and Sonoma.

Central Valley region: Escalon, Fresno, Kern, Kings, Livingston, Lodi, Madera, Merced, Modesto, the San Joaquin Valley, Stanislaus, Stockton, and Tulare.

Southern Coastal region: Cucamonga, Escondido, Ontario, Riverside, San Bernardino, Santa Barbara, and the San Fernando valley.

887

How many wineries are there in California?

About four hundred. These vary in size from a Northern Coastal enterprise with a capacity of a few thousand cases a year to a Modesto colossus that produces upwards of twenty million cases annually.

888

Can vinifera grapes be grown anywhere else on the West Coast?

Yes. Washington's Yakima Valley appears to be a viable area for such cultivation. Some experimental growths have turned out surprisingly well, and efforts in this direction are being expanded.

889

Can labrusca grapes be cultivated in Washington?

Yes. Some labrusca acreage has been successfully planted near Puget Sound. This is one of the few areas west of the Great Lakes where such experimentation has been fruitful.

890

What is Island Belle?

A red grape species that blooms in the state of Washington.

891

What is Muscadine?

A native vine family that inhabits the Southern states. The Muscadine strain grows almost wild, requires virtually no tending, and resists crossing with other stock.

892

What is James?

A member of the Muscadine family found in the Southern states.

893

What is Mish?

A wild white grape variety native to the Southern states.

894

What is Cynthiana?

A grape variety indigenous to Arkansas that yields a full-bodied, somewhat sweet red wine.

895

What is Scuppernong?

A wine made from Muscadine grapes. Scuppernong is a heavy, sweet amber wine.

896

What is Fredonia?

A grape variety native to New Jersey. Fredonia bears a passing resemblance to Concord.

897

What is Noah?

A semi-dry white wine made from a grape species native to New Jersey.

898

What is Ripley?

A white labrusca hybrid growth developed in New York State. Ripley is a trifle too bland to stand on its own. Further research is now being conducted to give Ripley a more assertive character.

899

What is Alpha?

An experimental red American hybrid grape strain. Alpha can withstand freezing temperatures but has a little too sharp an edge for widespread commercial use in its present state.

900

What is Missouri Riesling?

A white grape variety found in the Midwestern and Northeastern states. It is in no way associated with the European or California Riesling.

901

Is there anything unique about the vineyards of Ohio?

Yes. Most of them are situated on islands in Lake Erie. The major sites are North Bass and South Bass islands.

902

What is Ohio's predominant variety?

Catawba accounts for perhaps 90 percent of Ohio's harvest.

903

Do grapes grow in Michigan?

Yes. The southern part of the state is conducive to Catawba, Concord, and Delaware cultivation.

904

Is Illinois a wine center?

Not from an agricultural standpoint. However, one of America's larger suppliers is headquartered in Illinois. The wines under its brand name are made and packaged elsewhere.

905

What is New Jersey's viticultural profile?

Vineyard acreage is minimal, but packaging volume is very high. A leading brand of American Vermouth is processed and bottled in New Jersey. In addition a giant California supplier ships in bulk to New Jersey, where the merchandise is packaged for distribution to Eastern markets.

906

What is Maryland's claim to viticultural fame?

Although its production is nominal, Maryland has been active in French-American hybridization.

907

Why is the Finger Lakes district of New York State so named?

The district is dominated by several bodies of water whose composite layout is suggestive of the fingers of a human hand. These lakes include Canandaigua, Cayuga, Skaneatcles, Keuka, and Seneca. The Finger Lakes district is 250 miles northwest of New York City.

908

What are the key towns of the Finger Lakes district?

Canandaigua, Hammondsport, Naples, and Penn Yan.

909

What are the other wine districts of New York State?

1. The Hudson Valley—along the Hudson River seventy miles north of New York City. Clintondale, Highland, Marlboro, and Washingtonville are wine centers.

2. Chatauqua—below Buffalo along the shores of Lake Erie. Fredonia and Westfield are wine centers.

3. Niagara—above Buffalo in the direction of Lake Ontario. Lewiston and Model City are wine centers.

910

What is phylloxera?

A plant louse that can devastate grape vines. Labrusca vines have a natural immunity to phylloxera. Vineyard plagues have been put down throughout the world by grafting labrusca vines to infested vines in a way that combats the phylloxera without allowing the infested vines to take on any other labrusca properties.

911

Are all labrusca grape varieties identified with New York State bottlings?

No. Catawba, Concord, Delaware, Diamond, Dutchess, Isabella, and Niagara frequently are. Ives and Vergennes sometimes are. Clinton, Diana, Elvira, Iona, and Norton rarely are.

912

Do all labrusca grapes exhibit the same degree of foxiness?

Not quite. Concord's is the most accentuated. Catawba's is next. The others are somewhat less pronounced, although none is completely free of foxiness.

913

Which labrusca variety is considered New York State's choicest?

Without question—Delaware. Delaware is a white grape whose delicacy and finesse put it on a par with most of California's viniferas. It is the least foxy of any labrusca.

914

May a New York State Concord wine be artificially sweetened?

Yes. Artificial in this sense implies sweetness not derived from the wine itself. There is a broad consumer demand for Concord wine with an extra dimension of sweetness. Sugar is the sweetening agent.

915

What is New York State Málaga wine?

A rich, very sweet red wine made principally from Concord vinestock.

916

May water be used in making New York State wine?

Yes. Occasionally a pressing may show signs of excessive acidity. In such cases it is permissible to add a moderate amount of water to the juice during fermentation. The finished product, however, may not be treated in this manner.

917

What liquid may be added to New York State wine after fermentation?

The fermented beverage may be blended with wine made elsewhere. California wine is used for this purpose. The legal ratio is set at a maximum of one part California wine to three parts of New York State wine. A New York State wine may not be labeled as such unless at least 75 percent of its content is of New York origin. In practice the majority of New York State bottlings far exceed this requirement.

918

Do Concord and Catawba wines call for long vatting periods?

No. Both wines are ready for consumption soon after fermentation.

919

If New York State champagne is made mainly from Catawba grapes, why does it not always have a distinctly foxy after-taste?

For two reasons. New York State sparkling wines are made largely—but not exclusively—from Catawba grapes.

Premium bottlings combine Catawba juice with Delaware and other less foxy juices. The *cuvée* is thus somewhat moderated. Moreover, the juice undergoes a second fermentation and an aging period before final bottling. These steps aid in reducing Catawba overtones.

920

How successful has New York State been in cultivating European grape varieties?

In this connection any success at all must be regarded as monumental. It was thought for a long time that vinifera cuttings simply would not take root in New York State. This theory has now been discredited. After years of painstaking research two significant accomplishments have been recorded in the Finger Lakes district. A major winery has cultivated a few acres of Johannisberg Riesling and Pinot Chardonnay, and a small winery devoted to estate bottling of vinefras has been established. Among its list of vinefras are Johannisberg Riesling, Gewürztraminer, Gamay, and Pinot Noir. Prices are four to seven dollars a bottle.

921

Has New York State succeeded in crossing labrusca stock with French vines?

Very much so. Exhaustive work has been done with grafting and fusing native vines with vines from Bordeaux and Burgundy, Out of this effort has come an inventory of French-American hybrid varieties of high caliber. As a result the production of fine New York State table wines has been appreciably upgraded.

922

What is Baco?

A French-American hybrid species that vinifies into an excellent red table wine called Baco Noir.

923

What is Seyve-Villard?

A French-American hybrid group. The most popular Seyve-Villard bottling is Seyval Blanc, a crisp white wine.

924

What is Seibel?

A French-American hybrid family. One or another of the Seibel species may create a charming rosé, a top-notch red, or a lovely white.

925

What is Aurora?

A semi-dry white wine made from a Seibel offshoot.

926

What is Chelois?

A full-bodied red wine made from a Seibel offshoot.

927

What is Chancellor?

A French-American hybrid strain that yields a distinguished red wine.

928

What is Foch?

A red French-American hybrid wine of agreeable character.

929

What is Verdelet?

A French-American hybrid variety that produces a pleasant white wine.

930

How are the members of a French-American hybrid family identified?

In the trade, the family is named for the experimenter —Maurice Baco, Louis Seibel, etc. The members within a given group go by numbers—Seyve-Villard 5276, Seibel 5455, etc.

931

How much of New York's acreage is devoted to French-American plantings?

Less than 5 percent, virtually all of which is confined to the Finger Lakes district.

932

Must a New York State wine be made entirely from the identifying grape variety?

No. As with California varietals, the concept of the principal ingredient applies. In New York State practice, however, the identifying variety often represents 100 percent (or nearly 100 percent) of the content.

933

Is it permissible to call a New York State wine a varietal if the established criteria are met?

There is no law against it. The designation has lately come into broad usage by itself or in conjunction with the term "native American."

934

Do fine New York State table wines require as much barrel aging as those of California?

Not quite. Generally speaking, most New York State offerings seem to be more enjoyable when they lean toward the young, fresh side. The primary reason is the comparatively low level of tannin. The majority of the reds are mature enough for bottling within a year and a half. The whites are ready a little sooner.

935

Does New York State make any dessert wines to speak of?

Most assuredly. The Finger Lakes wineries consider Port and Sherry an integral part of their line. One supplier, in fact, maintains a superb solera system.

936

How do New York State and California wines compare in price?

Most New York State wines run from $2.00 to $2.50. Concord and Catawba may be less expensive. Wines from the Southern Coastal and Central Valley regions of California are usually in the $1.25 to $2.00 category. Northern Coastal generics are basically $2.00 to $3.00 wines; varietals may run double and triple those amounts.

937

How much U.S. wine is of New York State origin?

Between 8 and 10 percent.

938

How much U.S. wine is of California origin?

More than 85 percent.

939

Do California and New York State both produce brandy?

No. California does, but the distillation of grape juice is prohibited in New York State.

940

How much wine does the average American adult consume?

Approximately two gallons per year. If wine consumed in pints by derelicts were deducted, the figure would be substantially lower. The statistical imbalance is best illustrated by noting that the intake of only one pint per day (a conservative estimate for a "pint-drinker") would amount to a yearly consumption of more than forty-five gallons.

941

How does wine consumption in the United States compare with that of the largest wine-consuming countries?

The disparity is striking. Although we are now drinking twice as much wine as we did a generation ago, the French, Italians, Spanish, Portuguese and Argentineans drink ten to fifteen times as much wine as we do on an adult per-capita basis. In these countries wine consumption is a tradition of long standing. A glass or two of wine is looked upon as a natural and necessary accompaniment to lunch and dinner.

942

How many countries have an adult per-capita wine-consumption rate at least double that of the United States?

At least twenty-one. The five previously mentioned countries, plus the following sixteen, where it is known that the rate is from two to twelve times as great as our own: Australia, Republic of South Africa, U.S.S.R., Czechoslovakia, Belgium, West Germany, Bulgaria, Uruguay, Rumania, Yugoslavia, Greece, Luxembourg, Hungary, Switzerland, Austria, and Chile.

943

Which states exceed the national wine-consumption rate by at least 50 percent?

In order as follows: District of Columbia, Nevada, California, Oregon, Washington, Alaska, Vermont, Colorado, New York, Rhode Island, New Jersey, New Hampshire, New Mexico, Massachussetts, Arizona, Florida, Connecticut, Hawaii, Maryland, and Illinois.

944

Which states have a wine-consumption rate of less than half the national average?

Iowa, West Virginia, Alabama, Kansas, Kentucky, Tennessee, and Mississippi.

945

Which American age group shows the highest annual per-capita rate of consumption?

The eighteen- to twenty-nine-year-old group. Individuals in their late teens and their twenties drink an average of seven gallons of wine per capita, or more than three times the national average.

946

How do marketing experts explain the dominance of the young-adult market?

There is widespread agreement that wine (and beer)

223

seem to be more compatible than "hard" liquor with the more informal, casual, carefree social setting established by the eighteen- to twenty-nine-year-old group. The comparative economy of wine is also frequently mentioned.

947

How much of the wine, American and imported, sold in the United States costs less than $3.50 a bottle?

Almost 90 percent.

948

How much of the wine, American and imported, sold in the United States retails for more than five dollars a bottle?

Less than 4 percent.

949

Has the pattern of consumer taste preferences changed during the last decade?

Very much so. Sweet dessert wines, notably Port and Sherry, led the parade for more than three decades. Since the mid-sixties this category has declined from year to year. Table and "pop" wine currently outsell dessert wines decisively.

950

How do marketing experts explain this trend?

Marketing studies conclude that the switch to table and "pop" wines is part of a mass national trend toward lighter, milder alcoholic beverages. The same syndrome accounts for the five-to-one popularity of 80-proof vodka over 100-proof vodka and 86-proof bourbon over 100-proof (bonded) bourbon.

951

How much of the wine consumed in the United States is imported?

Slightly more than 16 percent, or just about one bottle out of every six.

952

What is the customs duty on imported wines?

Sparkling, crackling, and carbonated wines, $1.17 per gallon; still wines containing not more than 14 percent alcohol by volume, 37.5 cents per gallon; still wines containing more than 14 percent alcohol by volume, 21 cents to $1.00 per gallon, depending on type.

953

Which countries are the leading shippers to the United States?

In round numbers, Italy accounts for 25 percent of the imported wines sold here. France is next, with 22 percent, followed by Portugal and Spain, with 16 percent each, and Germany, with 10 percent.

954

Is any European wine imported in bulk?

A very small amount is received in barrels earmarked for selected restaurants, but no bulk shipments are handled for packaging, as is done with some cordials and whiskies.

955

What are the top five cities or metropolitan areas in consumption of imported wines?

New York (the five boroughs and Nassau, Suffolk, and Westchester counties), where 34 percent of all the wine consumed is imported; northern New Jersey, 28 percent; Washington, D.C., 27 percent; Greater Miami, 25 percent; and Chicago, 23 percent.

956

Which kinds of European wine are the top sellers in the United States?

The following all show a yearly volume of more than five hundred thousand cases: Beaujolais, Bordeaux (*rouge* and *blanc*), Chianti, French country wines (Midi), Lambrusco, Liebfraumilch, Portuguese Rosé, Rioja, Sangría, Spanish table wines (Catalonia), and Sherry.

957

What is a bonded American winery?

All American wineries are bonded. The term merely means that the premises have been officially registered by the federal government to facilitate the collection of excise taxes.

958

May a supplier make any therapeutic claims for his wine?

No. It is illegal to advertise or promote any brand of wine (or beer or spirits) as being curative or conducive to good health.

959

How good are the home wine-making kits sold in many stores?

They may be fun to play with, but wine, the finished product, leaves much to be desired. The ingredients and instructions that come with these kits will help in turning out, at best, nothing more than a flavored beverage.

960

Is it possible to make good wine at home?

Yes. However, the process calls for choice grapes, premium yeast, a good wine press, a serviceable barrel, excellent filtering apparatus, and strict hygienic controls.

961

How much wine is a private, unlicensed individual allowed to make at home?

The federal code states: "The tax imposed on wine does not apply to wine produced by the duly registered head of a family for family use and not for sale. . . . The quantity which may be produced . . . during a year may not exceed 200 gallons."

962

Are many wines too delicate to survive a three-thousand-mile ocean voyage?

This old canard has been debunked. Few wines are that fragile. Many delightful European wines seen here are extremely light-bodied and exceptionally low in alcohol content.

963

Why do some Americans who have visited Europe claim that some European wines taste better at the source than in the United States?

The reason is essentially psychological. The emotional atmosphere and the "romance" of the experience generate a momentary illusion out of proportion to the inherent properties of the wine itself. The reaction to the identical wine consumed at home is infinitely more detached and objective.

964

What is a kosher wine?

One made under strict rabbinical inspection attesting that the production facilities were immacutely clean (*kosher* means "clean") and were housed in a separate section of the winery. The latter provision, of course, does not apply if production is geared exclusively to kosher wines. Concord is the most popular type of kosher wine.

965

What is a jug wine?

A half-gallon or gallon bottle of reasonably priced table wine.

966

What is the robe of a wine?

Its color—for example, a rich robe, a deep robe, a pale robe, etc.

967

What is a flowery wine?

A light-bodied white wine with a clean, fresh, delicate bouquet sometimes bordering on a garden-like fragrance. Some of the better Moselle bottlings are flowery wines.

968

What is a flinty wine?

A dry, crisp white wine. Chablis is a flinty wine.

969

What is fleshy wine?

A full-bodied red table wine with "bigness" and depth of character. Châteauneuf-du-Pape and Barolo are fleshy wines.

970

What is a rough wine?

A full-bodied red table wine that has not yet reached its full maturity. There is an unmistakable note of premium grapes, but at the same time, the discerning palate senses that more aging is needed to develop the wine's smoothness and character. At two years a California Cabernet Sauvignon, for example, may still be markedly rough. At four years it may well be on the road to greatness.

971

What is a maderized (madeirized) wine?

A white table wine that has turned to a muddy-brown-looking liquid and has lost its pleasing properties. A slightly darker hue is no real cause for alarm; this may occur naturally with time and with no adverse effect upon the taste of the wine. One of the primary reasons for maderization is improper storage near a source of heat or sunlight.

972

What is an oxidized wine?

A table wine that has acquired an off-taste because of the seepage of air. A tiny opening in the closure of the bottle may be enough to cause the wine to become unpalatable as it sits on a store shelf or in a cabinet at home.

973

What is a spritzer?

A wine highball prepared by pouring three or four ounces of dry white wine into a tall glass containing ice cubes and filling with seltzer or club soda. A lemon twist may be added as a garnish.

974

What is mulled wine?

A wine cocktail that has gained popularity with enthusiasts of winter sports. Sugar, lemon, nutmeg, cloves, and cinnamon are added to a dry red wine. The mixture is then heated and served in a ceramic mug.

975

How long will a dry wine retain its taste appeal after the bottle has been opened?

A week at the most. As with a soda bottle, it is almost impossible to reseal a wine bottle with absolute hermetical tightness. Exposure to air—even a slight amount of seepage —will start to have a detrimental influence upon a dry wine after a few days.

976

How long will a fortified wine remain palatable after the bottle has been opened?

Even a poor one will keep for up to a month. The high alcohol content slows down the damaging influence of exposure to air. A well-made fortified wine—one that underwent a long vatting period and was infused with fine brandy—may be unimpaired after a year.

977

What is a carafe wine?

The "house" table wine featured in a restaurant. This is usually a moderately priced offering. It is so called because the wine is often brought to the table in a carafe that holds several generous servings.

978

What is a sommelier?

A wine steward or wine captain in a restaurant. He may wear a key around his neck as a symbolic link with the days when prize selections were locked in a wine vault or cellar.

979

How much do most restaurants charge for a bottle of wine?

About double the retail price.

980

In cooking with wine, is alcohol imparted to the food?

No. The heat of the oven or skillet causes the alcohol to exaporate rapidly. The wine acts as a flavor booster or intensifier without adding any "kick" to the food.

981

Is there a difference between cooking wine and drinking wine?

Yes. Cooking is sprinkled with salt. The purpose is to discourage on-the-job imbibing by kitchen employees.

982

What sort of wine goes best with what sort of main dish?

As a general rule a dry or semidry wine is best suited to accompany an entrée—a red for a robust dish or red meat such as steak or beef; a white for veal, lamb, poultry, fish, or seafood; a rosé for any kind of entrée. A wine that is too sweet may tend to be too overpowering for the main course, although it should be noted that some people find this combination satisfactory.

983

What type of main courses are not particularly compatible with wine?

Those which are heavily pungent, spicy, garlicky, peppery, or vinegary. These taste accents may tend to undercut or "kill" the taste of the wine.

984

How may a fortified wine be best served at the dinner table?

As a pre-dinner cocktail. Dry Sherry, Vermouth (sweet or dry or half and half), or a prepared aperitif are good choices. In place of a dessert or as a finale, Cream Sherry or Port are appropriate.

985

What kind of wine goes best with what kind of cheese?

One person may find Sherry to his liking with Edam cheese; another, Port; still a third, Burgundy. Interestingly enough, all are right. There are no categorical or definitive answers when it comes to wine-and-cheese combinations. The ultimate answer is dictated by one's own taste preferences. Experimenting with different cheese-and-wine combinations can be fascinating.

986

Should red table wines be served cold?

This issue engenders widespread disagreement. In some quarters it is deemed almost sacrilegious to chill a light-bodied red wine for more than a half hour or to present a full-bodied wine at anything except room temperature. The hard evidence to support this position is meager. It simply is not true that a red table wine is unfavorably affected by refrigeration. Quite the converse, the vast majority of such wines taste better cold. Despite the hue and cry raised in some trade circles, the American people prefer red table wines chilled.

987

How cold should rosés and white table wines be when served?

All rosés and most white table wines are at their most enjoyable when presented cold. Whites that are more sweet than dry (high-bred French Sauternes and classic German *"lese"* wines) may be more satisfying when brought out only slightly chilled.

988

Should a fortified wine be consumed at room temperature?

There was a time when it would have been unthinkable to drink, say, a Sherry any other way. There has been a marked trend toward drinking pre-dinner aperitif and dessert wines "on the rocks."

989

Are some wines ideally served in a pitcher filled with ice cubes?

Yes. Sangría gained tremendous popularity in this manner. Many people have since adopted the same idea for Concord, Catawba, and flavored and "pop" wines.

990

Can chilling a wine suppress its faults?

There is a notion that coarseness, bitterness, sharpness, or harshness can be temporarily reduced if the wine is served ice cold. This contention is a fallacy. A poor wine is a poor wine, whether it is drunk at room temperature or after being refrigerated for hours.

991

Does wine freeze at the same temperature as water?

No. Wine has a lower freezing point because of its alcohol. Water freezes at thirty-two degrees Fahrenheit; wine, at twenty-five to twenty-eight degrees.

992

How necessary is it to store a corked bottle of table wine horizontally?

Under certain circumstances it is advisable. If the wine is expected to remain unopened for more than three or four years the cork should stay moist. A dry cork may start to shrink as time goes on; air may trickle in, and the wine may become oxidized.

993

Why do some expensive red table wines have a somewhat unpleasant odor when the bottle is uncorked?

Because of the presence of tannic acid, an indispensable agent in maturation. As the wine continues to improve in the bottle, the tannin may give off a bit of a stale, stagnant odor when the bottle is uncorked. This offense to the nostrils is momentary and should not be viewed with alarm.

994

What is meant by letting a table wine "breathe"?

Exposing a musty wine (especially a well-aged dry red) to air to restore its bouquet. The oxygen in the air will begin to have a beneficial influence after a few minutes. It is a good idea to uncork a long-lived red table wine ten or fifteen minutes before it is to be poured. Time permitting, a half hour is even better. It may also help to allow the wine to "breathe" in the glass for five or ten minutes before it is consumed.

995

What is meant by decanting a wine?

Pouring the wine slowly from the original container into a server. Wines aged in the bottle may cast a small measure of natural sediment. Keeping the sediment from entering the wine glass can be readily done if the liquid is decanted in an easy gentle, steady motion. The deposit will usually settle at the bottom of the bottle. A fast, jerky movement may agitate the sediment toward the neck of the bottle and probably into the wine glass.

996

Is there a sure method to prevent cork particles from falling into the wine when the bottle is opened?

No. This will occur sometimes regardless of the type of corkscrew used (lever, wing, straight pull) or the care with which the corkscrew is inserted and manipulated. If a cork chip winds up in the glass, simply scoop it out.

997

Should different kinds of wine be served in different kinds of glasses?

It depends on how much of a fetish or ritual you want to make out of serving wine. Actually only two precautions really need to be observed. First, do not use a tiny or skimpy glass (cordial or jigger type). Minimum capacity should be four ounces. Fill only partially if just a sip or two is desired. Second, do not use a frosted or tinted glass. The color of the wine has sensory appeal.

998

Why do some wine buffs insist that table wine be served in oversized stemmed glassware?

So that the hand can be kept away from the bowl. It is maintained that the fingers should not obstruct the view of the liquid, that the wine should not be subjected to the heat of the palm, and that the glass should be no more than half-full to enable the wine to be swirled. How much homage should be paid to this rule is purely subjective.

999

How frequently do mislabeling violations occur?

Only once in a great while. During the past five years two incidents have been brought to light. In the first a California winery was fined for selling to an airline a quantity of varietal wines below the prescribed standard. In the second a consignment of Bordeaux wine was confiscated when part of the shipment was discovered to be from a lesser district.

Is it necessary to swallow a wine to judge its taste?

No. The throat and esophagus have no sensory acuity. The taste centers are in the lips, tongue, cheek walls, and the roof of the mouth. The structure of a wine can best be judged by tripping it over the tongue and rolling it around in the mouth. When a professional taster is called upon to evaluate a number of samples during a day he will rarely ingest the wine. Instead, he will eject the wine from his mouth into a bucket or sandbox.

1001

Do professional wine people have keener taste buds than laymen?

Absolutely not. Anyone with a normal sense of taste has the innate capacity to differentiate between an excellent wine and an inferior one. The ability to make fine distinctions comes naturally with exposure to different wines over a period of time.

Index

241

244

250

252

Wallufer Mittelberg, 107
Wallufer Walkenberg, 107
Washington (state) wines, 211
Wawern, 112
Wawerner Herrenberg, 113
Wehlener Klosterlay, 110
Wehlener Lay, 110
Wehlener Nonnenberg, 110
Wehlener Sonnenuhr, 109, 121, 122
Weingut, 117
Weinkeller, 117
White Pinot, 207
Wiltingen, 112
Wiltingener Braune Kupp, 112
Wiltingener Gottesfuss, 113
Wiltingener Klosterberg, 112
Wiltingener Kupp, 113
Wiltingener Schwarzberg, 112
Winche, 112
wine(s), 13
  acid compounds in, 17
  additives in, 27
  aging of, 22-23
  alcoholic content of, 13-14, 19, 26, 32, 88, 101
  "bottled by," 39
  "bottled for," 39
  bottle shapes, 98, 119-20, 142, 202
  bottling requirements of, 38-40
  carafe, 231
  with cheese, 232
  clean, 40
  color additives in, 16
  color classification, 15-16
  cooking, 231
  cooking with, 231
  cooling of, 233-34
  crackling, 134
  decanting of, 235
  dessert, 19, 20, 21, 159-60, 161, 165, 175, 179, 184, 185, 194, 196
  dinner, 199
  dry, 15, 21-23, 230
  estate-bottled, 38

Wine(s) *(cont'd)*
  federal taxes on, 32, 123, 134, 226, 227
  fining of, 29
  flavoring agents in, 27, 135, 161
  fleshy, 229
  flinty, 228
  flowery, 228
  with food, 232
  fortified, 19-20, 21, 40, 230, 232, 233
  fruit-flavored, 27, 182, 186, 189, 190, 197
  generic, 27, 34
  glassware for, 236
  "grand vin" labeling, 46
  home winemaking, 226-27
  jug, 228
  kosher, 228
  labeling of, 32, 36, 38-40, 80, 96, 114-18, 122, 125, 140, 161, 162, 167, 170, 186, 202, 217, 236
  "made and bottled by," 39
  maderized, 229
  measures of, 30-31, 142
  mesa, 171, 174
  metric measurements of, 31
  monopole labeling, 47
  mulled, 230
  oxidized, 229
  pasteurized, 29
  per capita and marketing statistics, 222-26
  "pop," 28, 234
  "produced and bottled by," 38
  proprietary, 30
  red, 15, 16, 17, 22, 23, 38, 40, 233, 234-35
  removal of impurities in, 29-30
  robe of, 228
  rosé, 15, 16, 17, 98, 134, 151, 176-77, 226, 233
  rough, 229
  sparkling, 125, 131-36, 147-48, 152, 186
  "specially selected," 39-40

This book was set in Linotype Electra
by Sweetman Typesetting Corporation